Dorothy

101 BEST-LOVED PSALMS, GOSPEL HYMNS, AND SPIRITUAL SONGS OF THE AFRICAN-AMERICAN CHURCH

Gwendolin Sims Warren

Ev'ry Time I Feel the Spirit

An Owl Book
Henry Holt and Company
New York

Henry Holt and Company, LLC
Publishers since 1866
115 West 18th Street
New York, New York 10011

Henry Holt® is a registered
trademark of Henry Holt and Company, LLC

Published in Canada by Fitzhenry & Whiteside Ltd.,
195 Allstate Parkway, Markham, Ontario L3R 4T8.

ISBN 0-8050-4411-6

Henry Holt books are available for special promotions
and premiums. For details contact: Director, Special Markets.

First published in hardcover in 1997 by
Henry Holt and Company, Inc.

First Owl Books Edition 1999

Designed by Betty Lew

Printed in the United States of America
All first editions are printed on acid-free paper. ∞

1   3   5   7   9   10   8   6   4   2

This book is dedicated with love to:

My father, the late Rev. Yancey Lee Sims, and my mother, the late Mrs. Anna Beach Sims, for their admonition, exhortation, and inspiration to follow Jesus.

My daughter, Maya Anna Warren, and my son, James Walter Warren Jr., for their sacrificial love and faithful support as I heeded the Call.

My God, for His faithfulness and strength: "I waited patiently for the Lord; and He inclined unto me, and heard my cry. He brought me up also out of an horrible pit, out of the miry clay, and set my feet upon a rock, and established my goings. And He hath put a new song in my mouth, even praise unto our God: many shall see it, and fear, and shall trust in the Lord" (Psalm 40:1–3, AV); "The Lord is my strength and song, and is become my salvation" (Psalm 118:14, AV).

Contents

II. The Gospel Songs   103

*Gospel Hymns, Historical Gospel, and Traditional Songs,
Songs of Tindley, Dorsey, Campbell, and others, 1870–1960*

III. The Euro-American Hymns   191
Hymns of Watts, Wesley, Crosby, and others, 1600–1950

Acknowledgments

I thank God for those who have gone before me, walking in the faith in spite of peril, dangers, and tribulations.

I praise God for my eighty-five-year-old Aunt Lillie and ninety-seven-year-old Miss Johnnie, both of whom are still trusting Jesus.

My thanks to:

Lawrence Jordan, my agent, who helped to pull out the idea for this book.

Theresa Burns, my editor, for her long suffering and excitement.

Tracy Sherrod, my current editor, who saw the book to its completion.

Roland Ottewell, the copy editor, for his meticulous work.

Kathi Mills, my gracious rewrite editor, who literally worked miracles.

Jayne Skoog, for her many hours of through-the-night work, and her assistance on the computer, phone calls, and technical skills.

Cheryll Greene, for her assistance in the rewriting.

Mary Bell, for the valuable copies of her late mother's old gospel songs.

Frederick Bush, who exhorted (scolded!) and inspired me when I was almost faint.

The pastors of Allen A.M.E. Church, the Rev. Dr. Congressman Floyd H. Flake and the Rev. Elaine McCollins Flake, for the opportunity to "come full circle" as I continue to walk out God's vision and purpose for my life.

The members of Shepherd's Heart Fellowship Church, who hung in there when I couldn't be there; Donna Darkins, our ministry assistant; Arthur Freeman, our praise and worship leader; Emmanuel Suarez, our teacher—all of you who picked up the slack.

A host of family and friends who encouraged me, supported me, and "prayed me through."

Ev'ry Time I Feel the Spirit

Introduction

We African-Americans have been richly endowed with the gift of music. For over two hundred years it has made its mark not only on the black Christian church but on American culture as a whole. From the early days of the camp meetings during our enslavement to the present-day Sunday service, the lifting up of our voices in songs of praise to God has been for the purpose of celebrating our Lord's resurrection. We assemble together in community to share in that victory of resurrection over oppression in any form, whether it be injustice, discrimination, or poverty.

The ministry of music and its importance to our spiritual lives is, I believe, the direct fruit of the early African-Americans' torturous journey in this land. Torn from their homeland and forcefully transplanted to a strange new country where their basic human rights were stripped away and replaced by barbarous and shameful treatment, these remarkable individuals managed to survive as a race of people. Amazingly, they adopted their oppressors' religion, welcoming Christianity's message of a loving, forgiving God, despite the fact that they seldom saw that message lived out by those who claimed to believe it. The very circumstances that were meant to subject those enslaved and restrict and repress their cry of pain were instead used as vehicles to release songs of victory.

It has always been so. The most severe and adverse situations brought forth the greatest and most powerful songs. As in the first centuries of the Christian church when believers endured great persecution, singing not only sustained them but brought triumph in the midst of the most difficult circumstances. The apostle Paul, while sitting in prison with his back laid open from a beating and his feet in stocks, lifted his voice at the dark hour of midnight and sang praises to God. The result was not only a great deliverance for Paul but the conversion of his jailer. That same apostle Paul is the one who instructed the church to sing "psalms, hymns, and spiritual songs" to God and to each other.

African-American believers, from their earliest days in the Christian faith, adhered to that directive even as they endured torture, racism, prejudice, and discrimination. Out of the bondage of enslavement came the spiritual. Out of the depression of the 1930s came the great gospel songs. Out of the civil rights movement of the second half of the twentieth century have come the bold and beautiful freedom songs and contemporary gospel and praise songs. These songs that have become part of the black Christian tradition give praise and thanksgiving to God in all circumstances, expressing confidence in His loving care, no matter what the situation. As noted black historian W. E. B. Du Bois once described it, these songs express the viewpoint that "God is on the side of the oppressed."

In much the same way that our music sustained our forefathers and mothers as they struggled for release from physical and spiritual bondage, it continues to sustain and encourage each new generation. For that reason, I have attempted to pull together the stories behind 101 of the best-loved hymns, spirituals, and gospel songs of our people. Among my resources for this project were three primary hymnals, which were invaluable in my research and for which I am extremely grateful: *The African Methodist Episcopal Church Bicentennial Hymnal, The New National Baptist Hymnal,* and *Yes, Lord! The Church of God in Christ Hymnal.* (See page 359 for further information on these resources.) Still, narrowing my choices down to 101 songs was no easy task, as I personally have hundreds of favorites! In fact, when I started this book I had narrowed those favorites down to about 300— which, needless to say, still left me with a lot of eliminating to do. If you are at all familiar with African-American church services, you know what I mean. Our music runs the gamut from the "Hallelujah Chorus" from Handel's *Messiah* to such simple but lively choruses as "Glory, Glory, Hallelujah!" But, eventually, I was able to pare down my list to 101 songs, along with a story or anecdote regarding each of them. These very real and human stories will, I believe, deepen and enhance our understanding and appreciation of our musical heritage, preserving it for our sons and daughters, as those who have gone before did for us.

Who I am today is the result of the blending of my spiritual inheritance and my God-given black heritage. I was born into a family that believed that singing is as necessary for worship as breathing is for life. Perhaps that is one of the reasons I chose the title *Ev'ry Time I Feel the Spirit* for this book. For, you see, every time we felt the Spirit moving in our hearts—and that was often!—we sang. In fact, almost since I could talk, I've been singing. One of my first memories is of making my choir debut, at the age of four, at the St. James African Methodist Episcopal Church in Atlantic City, New Jersey. It was during the Sunday morning service, and because I was the youngest and smallest of the forty junior choir members, I was the first one to march down the aisle.

My knees shook and butterflies danced in my stomach as I imagined what seemed to me to be the longest walk of my life. Would I remember the words? Would I trip and fall? Would I do something to embarrass my-self—or my parents? But then, as the strains of that wonderful old hymn, "Take My Life and Let It Be," began to resound throughout the sanctuary, I took my first hesitant step and led the processional down the aisle to the front of the church. How grand I felt in my black robe with the white smock over it! And how relieved I was to finally make it to the choir loft and look down at my mother, smiling up at me as she mouthed the words to the remaining verses.

That was in 1944. I was the only child of my father, the Reverend Yancey Lee Sims, and my mother, Anna Beach Sims. As far back as I can remember, our church and our home were always filled with music—both singing and playing. I made my first recording when I was seven, featuring "Just a Closer Walk with Thee," one of the 101 songs included in this book. By the time I was nine I was playing piano for the junior choir and substituting for the regular organist-pianist of our church in Riverton, New Jersey. I made my solo singing debut at the Griffith Auditorium in Newark when I was twelve.

What a rich musical heritage I was blessed with! In some of my father's churches there were as many as five choirs, as well as gospel ensembles, quartets, and the like. I became well-schooled in such Euro-American hymns as Charles Wesley's, the "high church" musical liturgy of the African Methodist Episcopal (A.M.E.) Church, the gospel music of Thomas A.

Dorsey and the Martins, and the classical-style church anthems for solo and choral repertoires. Being born into such a church music tradition brought me exposure at a young age to great singers like Marian Anderson, Paul Robeson, Dorothy Maynor, Roland Hayes, the Wings Over Jordan Choir, and the Dixie Hummingbirds. It was not unusual that all of these gifted artists passed through my father's church, because in those days the black church was the most accessible concert hall for those artists who were barred by racism from ministering and performing on the concert stages of this nation. Indeed, even Marian Anderson herself, the world-famous contralto and one of the most incredible voices of the twentieth century, was barred by the Daughters of the American Revolution (DAR) in 1939 from singing in Constitution Hall in Washington, D.C. In response to this, Eleanor Roosevelt, wife of President Franklin Delano Roosevelt, withdrew her membership from the DAR. It was later arranged for Anderson to sing on the steps of the Lincoln Memorial on that Easter Sunday. She sang to over 75,000 people. The singer's quiet dignity and tremendous talent brought down the color barriers, and Constitution Hall later opened its doors to all. Anderson herself sang there several times after that. But because this sort of prejudice and opposition was common in those days, African-American entertainers and performers spent a vast majority of their time singing in churches across the country.

I too continued to sing and play piano and organ in my father's church and in other community congregations until I went away to Oberlin College in Ohio and, eventually, studied at the Akademie Mozarteum in Salzburg, Austria. A lot happened during those next years, including an international opera and concert career, which gave me the chance to meet, work, and interact with some of the greatest African-American singers and composers of our time. One of those was the famous Hall Johnson, a composer, choral director, and leading authority on the spirituals, who has been called the "dean of the spiritual arrangement" for his expressive and dramatic work. Also, during the time I lived in Europe, I sang in the opera and on concert stages in Austria, Germany, Italy, and Switzerland. With a performance ensemble of an African-American, an Englishman, and an Austrian, I toured Europe for the United States Information Agency, presenting the program "The Negro Speaks of Rivers." The program featured African-American music from the time of the plantation spirituals to twentieth-century and contemporary compositions.

Throughout the years, as a student, professional performer, university and college professor, lecturer, and minister of music, I have had a personal involvement with every song in this book. I have dealt with all kinds of music, both sacred and secular, from early music of the second century to baroque, classical, folk, jazz, spiritual, anthem, gospel, and contemporary. I have sung in concert halls, auditoriums, cathedrals, and storefront churches. And I am honored and humbled by every one of those appearances.

But now I feel I have come full circle, returning to my beginnings of singing in the church. I recently served as music minister for seven years at Times Square Church in New York City, a church of fifty nationalities and ethnic groups. Currently I am serving on the pastoral staff at Shepherd's Heart Fellowship Church in Manhattan and am Minister of Music at the Allen A.M.E. Church, an 8,000-member congregation in Jamaica, New York, which touches the community in the borough of Queens. A great deal of the music we have used in these churches consists of contemporary arrangements of field spirituals, as well as depression-era and modern or contemporary gospel songs.

In 1986, I founded the Center for Worship and the Word, Inc., which presents the ministry of music through praise and worship. Through my work with the center and also with various churches, I see God continuing to use music, as He has through the centuries, to bring healing and inspiration to the many individuals of these congregations. Never was this truth so vividly exemplified as it was on Thursday, March 6, 1997. This was a day of great loss—but it was also a day of great celebration. A van was carrying children to our Allen A.M.E. Christian School that morning when a freak windstorm uprooted a large tree. It fell on the van and took the lives of four of those precious young children, two of whom were members of the Allen congregation. It was heartbreaking, to be sure. But that night, as congregants came together for an already scheduled concert by the Fisk Jubilee Singers, I witnessed a miracle. These twenty-two young Spirit-filled students told us they had not come simply to perform for us; rather, they had come to minister to us in our loss. As we joined with those young people in singing songs of faith, hope, trust, and comfort, God's healing power began to flow. By the end of the service, many who had come in faithfulness, grieving their loss, left thanking and praising God. Then, at a funeral service a few days later, a woman whose daughter—her only child—had been among the four victims made her way to the front of the church. In one of the most moving and memorable experiences of my life, I listened to her voice rise sweetly and victoriously above her grief as she sang "It Is Well with My Soul."

Witnessing that sort of miracle, time and time again, being released through songs of praise and worship to God, is a great blessing to me personally. Because of having been so richly blessed, I now desire to bless others. And that is why I have written this book. My aim in *Ev'ry Time I Feel the Spirit* is to introduce—or reintroduce—the songs that have become staples in African-American church worship services, and to show the miracle-working power behind these songs.

Growing up, I remember singing as many hymns by white composers such as Wesley, Watts, and Newton as I did black gospel music and spirituals. In fact, it was quite a while before I realized that such hymns were not exclusively A.M.E. songs. I have even heard about black colleagues of mine who, having also grown up in the church, believed that songs such as "All Hail the Power of Jesus' Name" and "It Is Well with My Soul" were "our" songs, only to find out that they were written by white English and American composers. For certain, many blacks have thought that "Amazing Grace" was a song authored by a fellow African-American. What a shock to learn that such a beautiful hymn was penned by a former slave trader! And yet, what a perfect example of the universal appeal of these sacred hymns and songs. Though the 101 selections included in this book are favorites of the African-American church, they are not exclusive to our race. These are songs that speak to the hearts of people from all cultures and races, of all ages, and from all eras of history. They are songs that heal, encourage, strengthen, reminisce, and excite. They are timeless, they are powerful—and they belong to everyone who will embrace them.

On the other side of the coin, there are some songs and hymns that have been sung in white churches and communities for years that are actually of black authorship, often unbeknownst to the congregations. Two primary examples are "I Bowed on My Knees and Cried Holy," by Nettie Dudley Washington and E. M. Dudley Cantwell, one of the selections in this book, and "I'll Wear a Crown," by the Reverend James Cleveland. Unfortunately, due to the lack of proper copyright information and access to publishing houses, as well as the lack of availability of expertise in copyrighting, compiling, and documenting such authorship, quite a number of songs have not been appropriately credited to original songwriters and composers. There are, sad to say, many incidents of piracy of black spirituals, gospels, and hymns from black songwriters.

Ev'ry Time I Feel the Spirit is divided into four sections, though the distinctions among those sections are somewhat artificial. It is impossible to accurately categorize these songs by era or style, as both so frequently overlap. I have called the first section "The Negro Spirituals: Plantation Songs and Jubilee Songs," dating it from 1600 to 1870. This covers the period of time from when the first African-Americans were enslaved until Emancipation, just after the Civil War. The second section, called "The Gospel Songs: Gospel Hymns, Historical Gospel, and Traditional Songs," focuses primarily on the depression era, but covers the years from 1870 to 1960. "The Euro-American Hymns: Hymns of Watts, Wesley, Crosby, and others, 1600–1950" is the third section. As is obvious from the dates, these songs span the years from both previous sections. Finally, there is the fourth section, "The Contemporary Gospel Songs," which begins with 1960 and carries through to the present day.

To understand the way different types of music overlap, we must first understand what is meant by "oral tradition." Because people spoke before they wrote, most of the stories that have been handed down from man's early history were done so orally, from one generation to another. Africans, who were brought to this country against their will, have been especially involved in the oral tradition, passing down stories verbally, often in the form of songs. Those who were enslaved and worked in the fields "sang their stories," not only of their current life but also of their homeland, teaching the children who listened about a country and a way of life they would not otherwise know existed.

And that is the reason the spirituals can so seldom be attributed to one particular author. They are songs authored by a people and a time, not by individuals. They were passed down orally, often being added to and changed through the years. When the enslaved adopted the Christian religion, their faith naturally became the focus of their songs. But their songs were not limited to the spirituals. Many of the hymns written by white composers—particularly Isaac Watts and the Wesleys—were readily received by the enslaved, only to be "blackened" as African-Americans adapted the music to their own style and culture. This type of hymn became known as a meter hymn and is still very popular in black churches today.

As the Civil War came to a close and the enslaved were finally emancipated, the age of the spirituals ended. During the latter part of the nineteenth century, as the former slave with newly found freedom began a northern migration while others stayed in the familiarity of the South, a new type of hardship arose. Those in the South found themselves living, for the most part, among hostile whites who were angry because they had lost the war and the right to own slaves. African-Americans who moved to the North discovered that they were not nearly as welcome as they had hoped. Instead they had to compete against whites for jobs in companies and industries owned by other whites. Those enslaved had been set free—but racism and prejudice had not died. Out of that situation rose the beginning of what we call the historical gospel hymns. These songs flourished during the social and economic deprivations of the depression, beginning to make their way out of the churches and into the mainstream after World War II.

The civil rights movement of the late 1950s and 1960s brought a rebirth to many of the older songs, particularly some of the spirituals. "Oh, Freedom," included in this book, is one of the best-known examples. As blacks and whites came together to peacefully protest the ongoing disenfranchisement of an entire race of people, "Oh, Freedom" and other songs became their rallying point. These songs were often called freedom songs, and were the bridge between what we know as historical gospel and modern or contemporary gospel songs. The publicizing of the marches and protests brought a wider exposure to this type of music, and its popularity spread.

Today, modern gospel is again one of the most popular sounds in the music industry. I am grateful for that. But in the midst of its success, I don't want to see the history of black sacred music lost. Like my ancestors who preserved our heritage through the oral tradition, I would like to help preserve it through the written word. Each of these 101 songs has a history of its own; collectively, they have a heritage that I would like to share not only with other African-Americans but with all of humanity.

Most important of all, I want to help ensure that the focus of this music—the God who carried my people through the good times as well as the bad—is glorified. Because that is what my life is about. I want to lift my voice in praise and thanksgiving for what God has done for me and for so many others. As has been the case throughout the history of the African-American Christian church, I consider it a great privilege to come together with others to sing praise and worship to God. With an ever-present song in our hearts and on our lips, we are always excited to go to the house of the Lord. Won't you join me on this joyous journey as, in the words of the traditional song "This Is the Day," we enter His court with praise?

This is the day
The Lord has made,
This is the day
The Lord has made,
This is the day
The Lord has made,
I will rejoice, I will rejoice, I will be glad.

I'll enter His gates
With Thanksgiving,
I'll enter His courts
With Praise.

I.

The Negro spirituals

Plantation Songs and Jubilee Songs, 1600–1870

"Ev'ry time I feel de Spirit
movin' in my heart,
I will pray."

*T*he Negro spirituals, also referred to as slave songs, plantation songs, or jubilee songs, due to their origin and their tone of victory over adversity, were birthed in a fiery, painful time for African-Americans. It was a time of bitter enslavement in a land thousands of miles from their home. And yet these songs are so much more than deep, beautiful outpourings of despair. They are songs of "jubilee" because the enslaved, in the midst of their despair, found fortitude, hope, and faith in God. They are songs of survival that answered, for early black Christians, the Israelites' question in Psalm 137: "How can we sing the songs of Zion in a strange land?" In the midst of a strange land, hearts aching with homesickness and bodies aching with fatigue and physical punishment, the African-American believers sang their faith and, in the process, found the strength to survive. The songs are called "spirituals" because the authors based the lyrics primarily on biblical stories and concepts and believed the Spirit of God to be the source. The song "Ev'ry Time I Feel de Spirit" is a prime example of the origin of the spirituals—when the authors felt inspired and moved by the Spirit of God, they prayed, they sang, they composed.

Negro spirituals are true folk songs of the American experience, yet in a unique way. Most folk songs of other cultures and societies have been primarily secular, whereas the spirituals are sacred and religious. These spirituals cannot be attributed to individual authors, but to the musical and spiritual genius of the African-American people. The songs were carried far and wide by word of mouth, from generation to generation, often being expanded through the years. This method of preserving songs and stories is called the oral tradition. It was through the oral tradition that Africa's ancient history, culture, and religion were preserved. It was natural, then, that the earliest African-Americans would preserve the spiritual in the same way.

For more than a century this nation's sacred and popular music has been branching off the new musical road laid down by the folk spiritual song form. You can hear how gospel music is rooted in it and how choral music styles are indebted to it. You can see how blues, country, rock, soul, rhythm and blues, and jazz all borrowed from its character and feeling, its intricate rhythmic patterns, rich harmonies, black vernacular, vocal techniques, and performance styles. This music is a lasting gift to the Christian church and to the whole human family.

The early African-American church was divided into two main branches: the "visible" and the "invisible" church. The visible church consisted of black congregations of the white denominations, a few independent African churches, and some mixed congregations where black and white worshippers met together. But the true strength of the African-American church was found in the invisible church, where worshippers met in praise houses and cabins called "hush harbors." This invisible slave church was a place to call on God for help and strength away from the eyes and ears of slave holders. These brave worshippers, risking floggings and worse if discovered, did not let fear stop them from coming together. In fact, the danger only spurred on the words and music of the spirituals. Their songs burst forth and flowed from hearts seeking freedom and release from the God whom they saw as their only hope. Often, in an attempt to muffle their voices, the congregation would huddle behind soaking wet quilts and rags that had been hung to form a sort of tabernacle. Another way the worshippers avoided detection was to take an iron pot or kettle, turn it upside down, place it in the middle of the cabin floor or at the doorstep, then prop it up slightly to hold the sound. Sharing their burdens, testifying to their victories, "everybody's heart was in tune," declared an eyewitness, "and when they called on God they made Heaven ring."

Drawn from the Bible, hymns, African styles of singing, and their creators' aspirations, experiences, and circumstances, the spirituals spoke of this world and of the next. They addressed a passionate longing for freedom and justice, and also embraced the virtues of Christianity: patience, love, freedom, faith, and hope. The music's authors used the Old Testament extensively, feeling a real kinship with the enslaved Hebrews. They expressed their trials as well as their hope in such songs as "Go Down, Moses," included in this section, and "Didn't My Lord Deliver Daniel?" Their criticisms of American slavery were usually couched in such symbolic language.

In the invisible church, without musical instruments, the song leader set the standard. His or her job was to touch the souls of the congregation with the spiritual and emotional quality of the songs in order to commune with God. Back and forth, worshippers and song leader, by call and response, reached toward this spiritual experience. They would rejoice in song, bow down in prayer, and cry out until they would "fall out," or "get happy," as some called it.

In the world outside of the church, African-Americans used the spirituals as codes to express their secret and most dangerous hopes and desires. They also used the spirituals to communicate from day to day about meetings, worship services, and escape opportunities. Without understanding these double meanings it is impossible to get a complete sense of the significance of the spiritual as a way African-Americans resisted enslavement. Three of the songs in this spirituals section, "Swing Low, Sweet Chariot," "Go Down, Moses," and "Steal Away," contain these coded meanings. The invisible church was the black grapevine of news about abolitionism, slave revolts, and the Underground Railroad network. Its music was often used as the code and signal of the movement.

Spirituals possibly appeared as early as the 1600s, but they were first documented when they began to pour forth in the mid to late eighteenth century. Their development ended shortly after Emancipation. A collection of more than 6,000 spirituals created by enslaved African-Americans still survives today.

These spirituals fall primarily into three melodic groups. The first is the call-and-response chant (the main type, of direct African origin), as in "He Arose," "Ain't Got Time to Die," and "Wade in the Water." The second is the slow, sustained, long-phrase melody, which includes such haunting, unforgettable songs as "Deep River," "Nobody Knows de Trouble I've Seen," and "My Lord, What a Morning." The most popular type of spiritual—the one that used to be mocked by blackface minstrel entertainers—is the syncopated, segmented melody. This type of spiritual is usually in a fast tempo, which inspires a deep physical response, as in "Ev'ry Time I Feel de Spirit," "Glory, Glory, Hallelujah!" and "All God's Chillun Got Shoes." All of these spirituals are included in this section of the book.

When the slave regime ended, the development of the spontaneous folk spiritual did too. The spiritual that came to international acclaim, starting late in the last century, had traveled far from its hush harbor roots—all the way to the concert stage. The legendary performances of the Fisk Jubilee Singers were intended to raise much-needed funds for their university

from white audiences and donors. They were enormously successful, helping to make the arranged spiritual a permanent American musical art form.

Arranged spirituals became a beloved part of African-American choral
and solo stage repertoire following World War I. The first all-black professional choruses appeared, and composer-arrangers Hall Johnson and Eva
Jessye pioneered a movement to train performers in African-American
communities.

Because of the spiritual's unique ability to touch the human spirit, the
form has kept its power through the generations. It is still being sung in traditional ways in black denominational churches and on concert programs,
and is still studied in colleges and universities throughout the land. In the
last ten years especially, inventive arrangements have brought a modern
sound to the spiritual song—harmonically, rhythmically, and instrumentally.
Some of the more contemporary arrangers like Donnie McClurkin, Kirk
Franklin, and Kurt Carr have breathed new life into many spirituals.
Through fresh vehicles such as recordings and videos, the spiritual is reaching broader audiences who are feeling the age-old resonance of this music
in their lives. This gift of the Eternal Spirit, delivered through the suffering
and triumph of the African-American soul, continues to enrich the world's
musical inheritance.

Ain't Got Time to Die

Words and Music by Hall Johnson (1880–1970)
in the style of a Traditional Spiritual

Solo

1. Lord,— I keep so bus-y prais - in' my Je - sus,

Keep so bus-y prais - in' my Je - sus, Keep so bus-y prais-

Choir

Keep so bus-y prais - in' my Je - sus, Keep so bus-y prais-

in' my Je - sus, Ain't got time. 'Cause when I'm

in' my Je - sus, Ain't got time to die.

Chorus

'Cause— it takes all o' ma time,————
die. 'Cause——it takes all o' ma time,— To praise my Je-sus,

all o' ma time.————
All o' ma time—— To praise my Lord, If

I don' praise— Him de rocks gon-ter cry out,

"Glo-ry an' hon - or,   glo-ry an' hon - or!"

"Glo-ry an' hon - or,   glo-ry an' hon - or!" Ain't got time to   die.

Now, won't— you git   out o' my way,—————

Now, won't—you git   out o' my way,—————

Ain't got time to die. Now, won't— you git   out o' my way,— Lem-me

Git out— o' ma way!—

Git out— o' ma way!—

praise my Je-sus?   Out o' ma way,— Lem-me praise my Lord! If

I don' praise— Him   de   rocks gon-ter cry out,

"Glo-ry an' hon - or,   glo-ry an' hon - or!" Ain't got time to die.

"Glo-ry an' hon - or,   glo-ry an' hon - or!" Ain't got time to die.

2. *Lord, I keep so busy workin' fer*
    de Kingdom,
   Keep so busy workin' fer de
    Kingdom . . .
   Ain't got time to die.
   'Cause when I'm feedin de po', Hm,
   I'm workin' fer de Kingdom . . .
   Ain't got time to die.

3. *Lord, I keep so busy servin' my*
    Master,
   Keep so busy servin' my Master . . .
   Ain't got time to die.
   'Cause when I'm givin' my all,
    Hm,
   I'm servin' my Master . . .
   Ain't got time to die.

*C*omposer-arranger Hall Johnson wrote "Ain't Got Time to Die" in the style of a spiritual. It was premiered for solo voice and orchestra at Lincoln Center in 1966 (I was the soloist) with the Symphony of the New World, said to be the first racially integrated symphony orchestra. The Symphony of the New World afforded many capable and gifted musicians—who because of their race were banned from the major symphony orchestras— an opportunity to use their talents.

Mr. Johnson was meticulous in interpreting the spiritual, as I learned while preparing for the Lincoln Center premiere. During that time I spent several hours with him in his Manhattan apartment. Mr. Johnson, who at that time was in his eighties, coached me on the interpretation of the song. He worked with me on every nuance, demanding that I give just the right expression of the tone, rhythm, and accents of the text. He meticulously demonstrated how to articulate each word or syllable with a percussive effect, listening for a close-to-authentic rendering of the slave dialect.

Over his entire career Mr. Johnson was dedicated to preserving the spiritual. He included in his song album, which contained thirty spirituals, page after page of instructions on how to sing, play, and present the spiritual. His arrangements of spirituals have been enormously popular with concert artists and groups, helping to keep this vital song form alive. Among the thirty spirituals arranged for voice and piano by Hall Johnson were such well-known songs as "Swing Low, Sweet Chariot," "There Is a Balm in Gilead," and "Were You There?", all of which are contained in this section. Because of his meticulous and exciting arrangements of the spirituals—bringing to life the rhythms of the music, lyrics, and dialogue, as well as the dramatic expressions of the text—and the success with which they have been performed over the years, it is easy to see why Hall Johnson is considered one of the most important arrangers and musical directors of his period.

When I think of this song, I can almost visualize a scene in slavery days. "Keep so busy workin' fer de Kingdom" is what the itinerant preacher-evangelist of this song tells the brothers and sisters in the slave quarters as he goes from cabin to cabin. He lays hands on the sick, comforts the downcast, gives food to the hungry. It was not unusual for some slaves to be permitted to minister to the needs of their community. In this way the slave owners or overseers freed themselves from the responsibility of caring for the needy, sick, or afflicted. I imagine this figure as a "Sister Amanda," an A.M.E. evangelist, so busy serving her Master Jesus that she has no time to be fearful of the slave master who might try to stop her. She needs to do this work, she has no time to stop—not even time to die.

All God's Chillun Got Shoes

Traditional Spiritual

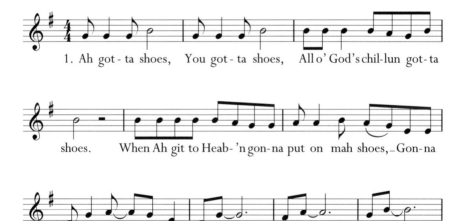

1. Ah got - ta shoes,   You got - ta shoes,   All o' God's chil-lun got - ta

shoes.   When Ah git to Heab- 'n gon-na put on mah shoes,—Gon-na

walk all ov - ah God's Heab-'n.—   Heab-'n,—   Heab-'n,—

Ev-'ry-bod-y talk-in' 'bout Heab-'n ain't go-in' dah.   Heab-'n,—

Heab-'n,———   gon-na walk all ov - ah God's Heab-'n.—

2. *Ah got a robe, you got a robe,*
   All o' God's chillun got a robe.
   When Ah git to Heab'n gonna
       put on mah robe,
   Gonna shout all ovah God's Heab'n.
   Heab'n, Heab'n, Ev'rybody talkin'
       'bout Heab'n ain't goin' dah.
   Heab'n, Heab'n, gonna walk all
       ovah God's Heab'n.

3. *Ah got a crown, you got a crown,*
   All o' God's chillun got a crown.
   When Ah git to Heab'n gonna
       put on mah crown,
   Gonna shout all ovah God's Heab'n.
   Heab'n, Heab'n, Ev'rybody talkin'
       'bout Heab'n ain't goin' dah.
   Heab'n, Heab'n, gonna walk all
       ovah God's Heab'n.

4. *Ah got a harp, you got a harp,*
   All o' God's chillun got a harp.
   When Ah git to Heab'n gonna
       take up mah harp,
   Gonna play all ovah God's Heab'n.
   Heab'n, Heab'n, Ev'rybody talkin'
       'bout Heab'n ain't goin' dah.
   Heab'n, Heab'n, gonna walk all
       ovah God's Heab'n.

5. *Ah got wings, you got wings,*
   All o' God's chillun got wings.
   When Ah git to Heab'n gonna
       put on mah wings,
   Gonna fly all ovah God's Heab'n.
   Heab'n, Heab'n, Ev'rybody talkin'
       'bout Heab'n ain't goin' dah.
   Heab'n, Heab'n, gonna fly all
       ovah God's Heab'n.

*S*pirituals have been collected by arrangers, scholars, and others inter-
ested in performing and preserving them, especially at the turn of the century and into the first four decades of this one. It was then that groups of
songs and some of the lore surrounding them were published. In attempts
to be "authentic," some of the song-origin stories contained awkward renditions of the Black English of the slavery period as well as stereotypical
depictions of African-Americans. Nevertheless, the tales sometimes give a
real feeling for how a song might have been created. In this case, the lore
associated with "All God's Chillun Got Shoes" involves Mary and her sons—

Tom, sixteen, and Joe, fourteen—all plantation field hands. Their story is recounted in a 1937 collection by composer William Grant Still and Ruby Berkley Goodwin. It goes something like this:

As far back as Tom and Joe could remember, Mary's blessing at the table had been, "Good Lawd, bless de victuals. Bless dese two boys an dey pappy. Keep me an de chillun togedder. Bless all God's chillun. Amen."

Tom had been wondering, and one day he asked hesitantly, "Mammy, who is God's chillun?"

"Why, we is, boy," she answered.

"But, Mammy, Uncle Jordan say dat God's chillun is blessed. He say dat God had ebberthin'. Sholy if we was His chillun He'd giv us somethin'. We jes' work, work, all de time. We don' neber hab nothin'. We ain't got no clo'es, ain't even got no shoes. Feet git pow'ful cold, an' de ground so hard."

"Wese God's chillun, too," his mammy answered him. "You wouldn't go on so ef you knowed what de good Lawd got fo' us."

"He got any shoes?" Tom was eager to know.

"Sho He got shoes. He got plenty shoes."

"When we gwinter git 'em?"

"When we git t' Heab'n," Mary answered with finality.

"Mammy, reckon ole head boss gwine to Heab'n?"

Slowly Mary said, "Everybody talkin' 'bout Heab'n ain't goin' dah."

"Ah got shoes an' you got shoes. We all got shoes," Tom and Joe said happily. "All God's chillun got shoes."

In the fields that day, Tom and Joe jested with the other hands. Soon the whole plantation was ringing with melody. As the song went down the field, Sis Carrie, "a singin' 'oman for true," as the people described her, took up the humble little song of joy and hope. "Ah got a robe," she sang. "Ah got a crown, you got a crown. All o' God's chillun got a crown. Ah got wings, you got wings. . . ."

Joe had never thought of that—with wings one could fly like a bird, like an eagle, like an angel—away up!

Joe was soaring when the commanding voice of the overseer brought him back to reality, but it was with a freed soul. And the best part of all was, "Ev'rybody talkin' 'bout Heab'n ain't goin' dah. Heab'n, Heab'n, gonna shout all ovah God's Heab'n." Still singing, Joe added, "Gonna fly all ovah God's Heab'n. . . ."

Amen

Traditional Spiritual

Chorus

1. A - men, Oh, Lawd - y! A - men, Have mer - cy! A - men, A - men, A - men. Sing it o - ver now. See the lit - tle ba - by (men.) Ly - ing in a man - ger On Christ - mas morn - ing. A - men, A - men, A - men, A - men, A -

3. *See Him in the temple*
   Talking to the elders,
   How they all marvelled!

4. *See Him at the seashore*
   Preaching to the people,
   Healing all the sick ones!

5. *See Him at the garden*
   Praying to the Father
   In deepest sorrow!

6. *See Him on the cross*
   Bearing all my sins
   In bitter agony.

7. *Yes, He died to save us*   8. *Hallelujah!*
   And He rose on Easter,   *Jesus is my Savior*
   Now He lives forever!   *For He lives forever!*

*I*n the Old Testament, the word "amen" means "sure, faithfulness, truly; so be it, truth." To say "amen" is to declare "I agree" with what has been said. Some may even say you can bet on it!

With that in mind, I can easily imagine the early African-Americans hearing a fiery sermon preached to them. Then, having been encouraged in the Lord, they begin to encourage the preacher in return with shouts of "Amen" and "Oh yes, oh yes, amen!"

In many of the hymnals of the historical Christian church, as well as in the African-American church, there are choral chants of the "amen." These are called the "Threefold Amen," the "Sevenfold Amen," and the "Tenfold Amen" (meaning the word "amen" is repeated three, seven, or ten times or more). Often these were sung with great fanfare at the end of the service, starting softly and building to a loud, exciting, majestic, resounding climax. These final "amens" signified agreement with all that had taken place. It had been established. So be it!

Some years ago, the gifted gospel songwriter Edwin Hawkins arranged this song, adding verses such as "See the little baby (Amen), on Christmas morning (Amen, Amen, Amen)!"

Grandma Johnnie was a stewardess in the church my father pastored in Princeton, New Jersey, in the 1960s, the Mt. Pisgah A.M.E. Church. She sat with me for hours one day, just talking about the Lord and her life with Him. We sat at the table in the kitchen where she had, at the age of ninety-six, cooked and set out some delicious dishes. We dined on crab cakes, baked chicken, cornbread, greens, and her famous sour cream cake. At one point, having meditated on the goodness of God, His mercy toward her, and His great faithfulness over those ninety-six years, she looked over at me with blazing eyes.

"Gwen," she said, "tell the people to trust in the Lord."

The dialogue between us continued, interspersed with the nodding of our heads in agreement and the repeated declarations of "amen."

Grandma Johnnie, who was a spinster, had an older spinster sister named Bea, who at that time was ninety-nine. Both had lived long enough to know that the God of their fathers could and would carry them through life. When I asked Johnnie about her history, she said she didn't know much about her ancestors. However, she explained, her grandmother lived in Virginia before coming to South Carolina. She had helped build the courthouse in Leesburg, Virginia. When General Lee came out of the army, Johnnie's grandmother had been a little girl. She had helped her mother prepare a big feast for him at the time. Johnnie also knew her grandmother had been born in Africa because she had always talked about when she came to the "new country."

"Oh, but she was a good Christian woman," Johnnie said of her grandmother. "She always talked to me and taught me about the Lord." Throughout the entire explanation of her background, she punctuated her thoughts with "amens," as if to say, "And that's the truth!"

Deep River

Traditional Spiritual

*T*he early generations of enslaved Africans lived with an intense desire to return home. In a few cases their dreams became reality, such as in Guilford County, North Carolina, where "Deep River" originated. Quakers there bought the slaves with the intention of getting them back to Africa. Paul Cuffee was a courageous African-American Quaker sea captain who made several trips in the early nineteenth century carrying many of these fortunate men and women home. Undoubtedly their desire for Africa was bound up in the image of the "campground" in this song. The image was often synonymous with the Promised Land, a temporal place where they could rest from their physical labors, a place of earthly freedom. Most often the campground referred to Heaven, an eternal place, where endless rest in the presence of the Lord was possible. In fact, in some of the earliest versions of the song, three final lines are added, speaking of the time when believers will finally have arrived in Heaven:

> *Walk into Heaven, and take my seat,*
> *And cast my crown at Jesus' feet,*
> *Oh deep river, Lord, I want to cross over into campground.*

"Deep River," like most other spirituals, contains multiple levels of meaning. In this case, besides its sacred aspect, its text gives it political significance as well, as do "Steal Away," "Didn't My Lord Deliver Daniel?" and "Roll, Jordan, Roll." Specifically, "Deep River" is a dual-coded song of the Underground Railroad. It was often sung to help map out a route to freedom, possibly indicating that escape would involve crossing a river in order to avoid the tracking of patrols and dogs.

Musically, "Deep River" was one of the spirituals with a characteristically sustained, long-phrased melody. It easily lent itself to the kind of arrangements that all-important composer-singer Harry T. Burleigh created in this century's early decades. His beautiful setting of "Deep River" in the style of an art song for solo voice and piano was the first of its kind. Burleigh, who was also a music editor for the international publishing house Ricordi, published the song in 1917. Among the many famous singers he coached were the Italian tenor Enrico Caruso and African-Americans Marian Anderson, Roland Hayes, and Paul Robeson. Robeson in particular made this song unforgettable as, with his rich, deep bass baritone, he carried his listeners to the very riverbed of the deep waters.

Ev'ry Time I Feel de Spirit

Traditional Spiritual

Fast
Chorus   *Fine*

Ev-'ry time I feel de Spir-it mov-in' in my heart, I will pray.

Solo or unison

1. Up on the moun-tain   my Lord spoke,   Out o' His
   In   de val - ley,   on my knees,   Ask my

D.C.

mouth came   fire and smoke.
Lord have   mer - cy please.

2. Jerd'n River chilly an' col',
   Chill-a de body but not de soul.
   All aroun' me look so shine,
   Ask my Lord if all was mine.

3. Ain't but one train runs dis track,
   It runs to Heaven an' runs right
      back.
   Saint Peter waitin' at de gate,
   Says, "Come on, sinner, don't
      be late."

The chorus of "Ev'ry Time I Feel de Spirit" describes the heart of the Christian experience that African-American people under slavery fashioned for themselves in their religion: communion with the Holy Spirit, prayer, and song. As the title song of this collection, it represents that essential spiritual grounding of African-American culture. It captures the feeling of the slave hush harbor services, when believers would gather, with their ingenious acoustical defenses in place, and become filled with the Holy Ghost.

"Sometime we come out of the field . . . scorchin' and burnin' up with nothin' to eat, and we wants to ask the good Lawd to have mercy . . ." remembered a slave named Richard Caruthers. "We takes a pine torch . . . and goes down in the hollow to pray. Some gits so joyous they starts to holler loud and we has to stop up they mouth. I see [people] git so full of the Lawd and so happy they draps unconscious." The song, a typical spiritual style, has a fast, vibrant tempo, full of accents and syncopation. It is this style that inspires and accompanies the singers' swinging, swaying, hand-clapping, dancing, and shouting.

By feeling the Spirit and praying in their own "invisible" church, in their own way, enslaved African-Americans defied slave owners who wanted to keep them ignorant of Christianity's message of deliverance and freedom. Of course, such messages underlie the spirituals as a whole. These songs often came as a result of revelations of the Spirit's work in life's circumstances and situations. This is where we get the term "spiritual songs," also referred to as "new songs" for the spontaneous way they would spring up. They were a direct answer to the apostle Paul's urging to "sing psalms and hymns and spiritual songs to God with thankful hearts."

It was this sort of spontaneous singing that lent itself to what is still known and practiced today, the "minstrel ministry." (This is not to be confused with the vaudevillian minstrel acts, where blackface performers mock the African-American spiritual.) In the Old Testament, minstrels were called upon to make music, singing and playing instruments. Often, as in the case of the prophet Elisha in 2 Kings, a prophet was in need of hearing from God. He would then call for a "minstrel," or singer, who would begin to sing and play what is termed an "anointed" melody, meaning a melody inspired by or touched by the presence of God. In turn, the music would inspire the prophet to hear and receive a message from God. The prophet (or preacher) would then speak forth that message, often in the midst of a song. In slavery days, the preachers would begin to moan, hum, and sing in order to stir up the gift within, seeking to receive revelation and illumination from God as they preached. As a result, preachers often ended up singing their sermons. Preachers still practice this ministry today, sometimes interrupting their preaching to sing a message from God. The instrumentalists—pianists, organists, drummers—join in, accenting and underlining the preacher's message. The minstrel ministry is a classic example of the ministry that flows forth "ev'ry time we feel the Spirit."

Ezekiel Saw the Wheel

Traditional Spiritual

1. Bet-ter mind, my sis-ter, how you walk on the cross,
'Way in the mid-dle of the air. Your foot might slip and your
soul be lost, 'Way in the mid-dle of the air.

2. *Let me tell you, brother, what a*
   hypocrite do,
   'Way in the middle of the air,
   He'll low-rate me and he'll
   low-rate you,
   'Way in the middle of the air.

3. *Ol' Satan wears a clubfoot shoe,*
   'Way in the middle of the air,
   If you don't mind, he'll slip it
   on you,
   'Way in the middle of the air.

*I*n its music and words, "Ezekiel Saw the Wheel" colorfully brings a part of the Bible to life. A favorite of jubilee choirs and singers in the post–Civil War era, when performed in a choral arrangement it was an exciting number. The various voices underlying the main melodic theme would indeed sound like wheels turning, like the wheel within a wheel.

The text, with its typical aspects of "deep biblicism," bases its lyrics on the Old Testament book of the prophet Ezekiel. The prophet, as he sat by the River Chebar, saw the glory of God in a heavenly vision. The song's chorus is taken from the first chapter of the Book of Ezekiel, where the prophet describes the vision containing the wheels.

It is not hard to imagine that the slaves might have identified in a special way with Ezekiel, who at the time he gave the prophecies was exiled from Jerusalem, a captive laboring in the wastelands of Babylon. He came from a priestly family of distinction and had been groomed to serve in the royal holy temple. Surely the New World Africans recognized in Ezekiel's plight many of their own number who had once been of high standing in their cultures and societies in Africa.

Speaking to one another in the three verses of the song, community members were "signifying"—insinuating, hinting, subtly indicting, and especially looking askance at the hypocritical slave holder or the betraying neighbor. The community was also strongly preaching "you gotta walk right" or "your foot might slip and your soul be lost." Watch out for the devil, they warn—he has a "clubfoot," a distorted foot that can trip you up, lead you astray so you can't walk the straight path. But—the genius of these song poets!—at the same time they are also contrasting the devil's crooked devices with the straight walking of the heavenly beings in Ezekiel's vision.

Give Me Jesus

Traditional Spiritual

1. Oh,— when I come to die, Oh, when I come to die, Oh,—
when I come to die, Give me Je - sus. Give me

Je - sus, Give me Je - sus, You may have all this world, Give me Je - sus.

2. *I heard my mother say,*
   I heard my mother say,
   I heard my mother say,
   Give me Jesus.

3. *Dark midnight was my cry,*
   Dark midnight was my cry,
   Dark midnight was my cry,
   Give me Jesus.

4. *In the morning when I rise,*
   In the morning when I rise,
   In the morning when I rise,
   Give me Jesus.

5. *I heard the mourner say,*
   I heard the mourner say,
   I heard the mourner say,
   Give me Jesus.

*G*ive Me Jesus" is a favorite song of Louvenia "Mom" Pointer, a preserver of the spiritual, now in her eighties. Mom Pointer has spent more than seventy years singing and living with the music created out of the slave experience. More than ten years ago she founded and continues to direct the Great Day Chorale in New York City to perform these songs and, in so doing, to preserve them. Mom Pointer and the members of the chorale are convinced that African-Americans survived the cruel, dehumanizing institution of slavery, emerging full of hope and faith, because they had this special song in their hearts. It is their belief that God turned the evil of the experience into the soaring gift of song.

Born out of pain, loneliness, and suffering, a song like "Give Me Jesus" could be a response to a commonplace tragedy like the brutal loss of children and other family and friends to the auction block. Persons in slavery, deprived and besieged in this life, might have nothing earthly to hold on to. But if they were Christians, they believed they had an inheritance in God. This song was sung not in sorrowful resignation but in confidence and in surrender to Jesus, who was their "All in All."

In talking with Mom Pointer, I asked her why this song was so meaningful to her and why, even in the midst of our conversation, it seemed to rise up from the depths of her soul. Her explanation was straightforward. "Anyone who knows Jesus knows that He's everything. If you've got Him, you've got everything. If you don't have Him, you don't have anything. I know what it is to wake up before day and sense His presence. I think of the many times when 'dark midnight was my cry, just before the break of day.' Oh, give me Jesus!"

Mom Pointer can still hear her own mother's deep and resonant alto voice seeming to reach up to Heaven with this beautiful spiritual's rich, uplifting melody. To such a solo line a chorus of voices would echo, "You may have all this world, Give me Jesus."

This song was the first published arrangement of African-American Edward H. Boatner, who also arranged such songs as "On Ma Journey," "Soon I Will Be Done," "Let Us Break Bread Together," and "Oh! What a Beautiful City," the last of which is also included in this spirituals section.

Glory, Glory Hallelujah!

Traditional Spiritual

1. Glo-ry, glo - ry,———— hal - le - lu - jah!————

——— Since I laid my——— bur - den down,————

Glo-ry,   glo - ry,——   hal - le - lu - jah!——

— Since I   laid   my——   bur-den   down.————

2. *I feel better, so much better,*
   Since I laid my burden down,
   I feel better, so much better,
   Since I laid my burden down.

3. *Feel like shouting "Hallelujah!"*
   Since I laid my burden down,
   Feel like shouting "Hallelujah!"
   Since I laid my burden down.

4. *Burdens down Lord, burdens down*
      Lord,
   Since I laid my burden down,
   Burdens down Lord, burdens down
      Lord,
   Since I laid my burden down.

5. *I am climbing Jacob's ladder,*
   Since I laid my burden down,
   I am climbing Jacob's ladder,
   Since I laid my burden down.

6. *Ev'ry round goes higher and higher,*
   Since I laid my burden down,
   Ev'ry round goes higher and higher,
   Since I laid my burden down.

7. *I'm goin' home to be with Jesus,*
   Since I laid my burden down,
   I'm goin' home to be with Jesus,
   Since I laid my burden down.

*I*magine African-American men and women, exhausted from sunup-to-sundown hard slave labor, singing themselves to exuberance—to life! This song of deliverance, of victory over emotional and physical oppression, served them well. After a night of "praying through" (praying until they felt they had touched the heart of God and been touched in return), they could lay down their burdens and face the next day with renewed strength.

How many times I have seen this truth lived out in worship services today! People, loaded down with the weight and burdens and sorrows of this world, come together in faith to praise and worship God. They are offering a "sacrifice of praise," a term which means to praise God regardless of circumstances, simply because He is God. They are then able to walk away from that time in His presence with the weight lifted and the joy of the Lord shining on their faces. They have literally "sung themselves to life."

Today this song is still one of the best-known spirituals, its popularity evident also in other churches. In fact, it is usually sung at least once a week in the average African-American church. It is performed in its original jubilee, or slave-era, style as part of the testimony service before the formal start of Sunday worship services. There, when congregants are expressing thanks to the Lord for having brought them through the week's events and circumstances, it reinforces their belief in God who hears and answers. At weekly prayer meetings it might be used as a "filler" during a lull when believers are in silent or audible prayer, waiting on the Lord. On Sundays, after a convicting sermon, and following the altar call, when worshippers have laid their burdens down and found relief, the pastor or a deacon may start this song. The congregation joins in, singing this message of repentance, relief, encouragement, and affirmation.

Go Down, Moses

Traditional Spiritual

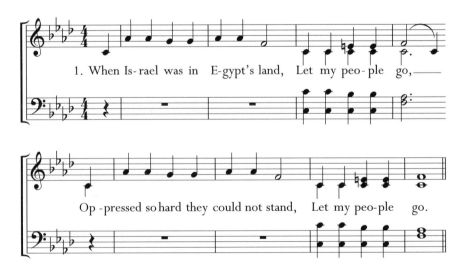

1. When Is-rael was in E-gypt's land, Let my peo-ple go, ——

Op-pressed so hard they could not stand, Let my peo-ple go.

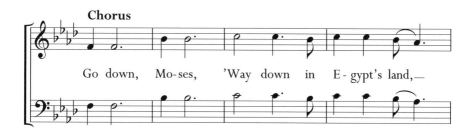

2. *Thus saith the Lord, bold Moses said,* . . .
   If not, I'll smite your first-born dead . . .

3. *No more shall they in bondage toil,* . . .
   Let them come out with Egypt's spoil; . . .

4. *When Israel out of Egypt came,* . . .
   And left the proud oppressive land, . . .

5. *Oh, 'twas a dark and dismal night,* . . .
   When Moses led the Israelites, . . .

6. *'Twas good old Moses and Aaron, too,* . . .
   'Twas they that led the armies through, . . .

7. *The Lord told Moses what to do,* . . .
   To lead the children of Israel through, . . .

8. *Oh, come along, Moses, you'll not get lost,* . . .
   Stretch out your rod and come across, . . .

9. *As Israel stood by the water side,* . . .
   At the command of God it did divide, . . .

10. *When they had reached the other shore,* . . .
    They sang a song of triumph o'er, . . .

11. *Pharaoh said he would go across,* . . .
    But Pharaoh and his host were lost, . . .

12. *O Moses, the cloud shall cleave the way,* . . .
    A fire by night, a shade by day, . . .

13. *You'll not get lost in the
wilderness, . . .
With a lighted candle in your
breast, . . .*

14. *Jordan shall stand up like a
wall, . . .
And the walls of Jericho shall
fall, . . .*

15. *Your foes shall not before you
stand, . . .
And you'll possess fair Canaan's
land, . . .*

16. *'Twas just about in harvest
time, . . .
When Joshua led his host
divine, . . .*

17. *Oh, let us all from bondage
flee, . . .
And let us all in Christ be
free, . . .*

18. *We need not always weep and
moan, . . .
And wear these slavery chains
forlorn, . . .*

19. *This world's a wilderness of
woe, . . .
Oh, let us on to Canaan go, . . .*

20. *What a beautiful morning that
will be, . . .
When time breaks up in
eternity, . . .*

21. *O brethren, brethren, you'd better
be engaged, . . .
For the devil he's out on a big
rampage, . . .*

22. *The devil he thought he had me
fast, . . .
But I thought I'd break his chain
at last, . . .*

23. *Oh, take your shoes from off your
feet, . . .
And walk into the golden
street, . . .*

24. *I'll tell you what I like the
best, . . .
It is the shouting Methodist, . . .*

25. *I do believe without a doubt, . . .
That a Christian has a right to
shout, . . .*

One of the most famous and favorite of all spirituals, "Go Down, Moses" depicts the Bible story of the exodus of the Israelites out of Egypt across the Red Sea. They were first led by Moses, and then Joshua, as they made their way through the wilderness into the Promised Land. As God's chosen people, the Israelites were mightily tested by the oppressing hand of Pharaoh. The song goes on to tell of the Hebrews' release from bondage, likening such freedom to the redemption of humanity through the suffering and victory of Christ on the Cross of Calvary. The parallels to the circumstances of the New World Africans in this alien land were quite clear to them. Because "this world's a wilderness of woe," the slaves were urged to seek earthly freedom from the white master, and at the same time to seek salvation. The message of the song is to shake off the yoke of sin, the chains of the devil, and be engaged in the army of the Lord, as a soldier of the cross.

This piece is a classic example of the double or coded meaning that is a key to understanding the lyrics and the role songs played in daily slave life. The song's creators majestically express the hope and desire that God send a deliverer to command the slave owners to "let the people go." Harriet Tubman, the great freedom fighter who was instrumental in smuggling many slaves out of the South to the northern United States or Canada by way of the Underground Railroad, used this song to call those slaves to freedom.

When that great day dawns, the song declares that "a Christian has a right to shout." The uniquely African-American "shout" is the believer's way of fervently praising and glorifying God in a very vocal and physical way, with all one's mind, heart, and soul. Such fervor was the reason the clever acoustical devices were used in the slaves' hidden church services, which sometimes went on all night. Today the same fiery expressions of devotion to and adoration of God are part of the African-American Christian's worship.

Go, Tell It on the Mountain

Traditional Spiritual

Go, tell it on the moun-tain, O-ver the hills and ev - 'ry-where,

Go,   tell it on the moun-tain That Je - sus Christ_ was   born.

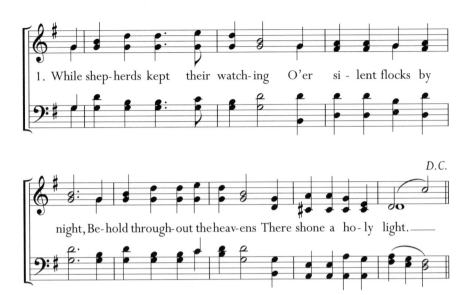

1. While shep-herds kept their watch-ing O'er si - lent flocks by night, Be-hold through-out the heav-ens There shone a ho-ly light.——

2. *The shepherds feared and trembled*
   When lo! above the earth
   Rang out the angel chorus
   That hailed our Savior's birth.

3. *Down in a lonely manger*
   The humble Christ was born,
   And God sent us salvation
   That blessed Christmas morn.

*A*s is true of most spirituals, we cannot pinpoint an author for "Go, Tell It on the Mountain." But we do know that it was adapted, arranged, and made popular by African-American composer John W. Work III. Unlike Hall Johnson, who later arranged many spirituals and meticulously instructed the singers and accompanists to keep to the original style and delivery of the spirituals, Work felt strongly that it was vital to "de-Africanize" the style to make them more appealing and acceptable to white listeners. By doing so, he hoped to hasten racial progress. To preserve the spiritual in its orig- inal state was, according to Work, to "doom it to stagnation and to the contempt of highly musical people." Yet even with today's contemporary styling, settings, and arrangements of the spirituals, the music seems to be returning to its original delivery, contradicting Work's beliefs.

Through the years scholars and others studying the spirituals have com- mented on the rarity of songs that tell of the birth and infancy of Jesus.

This is not surprising, since the Bible itself speaks more of the death and resurrection of Jesus than it does of His birth. But you can find occasional mentions of the birth in some of the spirituals, and there are some well-known Christmas songs that vividly depict the birth. Examples of those would be "Go, Tell It on the Mountain," "Dar's a Star in de East," "See the Little Baby, Born in the Manger," "Mary Had a Baby," and "Rise Up Shepherd and Foller." Noted early arrangers of the spiritual, Hall Johnson and Edward Boatner, effectively scored "Glory, Hallelujah to the New Born King" and "New Born!" respectively. In contrast, the Crucifixion and Resurrection have been depicted over and over again by the creators of the spirituals (see, for example, "He Arose," also in this section).

The famous song and musical-stage writing duo of the early 1900s, brothers James Weldon Johnson and J. Rosamund Johnson, published two collections of spirituals in the 1920s, giving attention to the somewhat puzzling absence of Christmas spirituals. One explanation James Weldon Johnson gives is that African-Americans preferred to think of Jesus as God, as almighty, all-powerful, rather than as an infant. In the older spirituals He is generally given a title of power, sometimes "Massa Jesus," most often "King Jesus."

Johnson says another reason may be that in the South the anniversary of the birth of Jesus was not a sacred or religious holiday. Even almost as late as the time of the publication of Johnson's book, Christmas in the South had been the most secular, even profane, of holidays, celebrated primarily with gunpowder and whiskey. In the slave era it was the one day when plantation slaves were allowed more freedom to come and go, when whiskey was distributed, and singing, dancing, and visiting took place. It may have been a conscious plan of the slavery establishment to make Christmas a day on which the enslaved, through sheer excess of sensuous pleasure, would forget their chains.

Johnson feels that the majority of the nativity spirituals in existence belong to a period some time after Emancipation, when a new idea of Christmas and of Christ developed. This is borne out by the absence of this type of song in the early standard collections.

Great Day! Great Day!

Traditional Spiritual

Chorus

Great__ day! Great day, the right- eous march- ing

1.   *Fine*

Great__ day! God's going to build up   Zi- on's   walls!

2.   Leader

1. Char - iot rode on the moun- tain top,

2.

God's going to build up Zi- on's walls!__

My— God spoke and the char-iot did stop,

God's going to build up Zi-on's walls!—

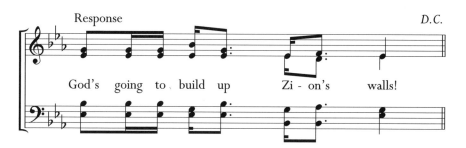

God's going to build up Zi - on's walls!

2. *This is the day of jubilee,*
   God's going to build up Zion's walls!
   The Lord has set His people free,
   God's going to build up Zion's walls!

3. *When I was a mo'ner jus' like you,*
   God's going to build up Zion's walls!
   I prayed an' prayed till I come
      through,
   God's going to build up Zion's walls!

4. *We want no cowards in our band,*
   God's going to build up Zion's walls!
   We call for valiant-hearted men,
   God's going to build up Zion's walls!

5. *Going to take my breast-plate,*
      sword, and shield,
   God's going to build up Zion's walls!
   And march out boldly in the field,
   God's going to build up Zion's walls!

*I*n the Old Testament, the "day of Jubilee" was the time when all Hebrews who had, for whatever reason, sold themselves into slavery, were released. When the African-Americans' day of Jubilee arrived after the Civil War, it was the greatest of days for the plantation slave community all over the South. But Emancipation arrived earlier in some places than in others. Union armies were routing the Rebels, who were in retreat.

The lore related to "Great Day! Great Day!" tells of a situation involving two African-American men, Jed and Chick. These men were caught sight of one night at the edge of a clearing by retreating Rebels, who were camped in the clearing between a swamp and a plantation. Jed and Chick and their band of men, women, and children had been holed up in the swamp, hiding from the approaching Confederates and waiting for the Union army to appear. The Rebels were blocking the slaves' path to the plantation's food supplies, and Jed and Chick had been searching out a way to get around them.

The little band of refugees who were camped at the dry place in the center of the swamp knew the soldiers would be looking for them as soon as the sun rose. They readied their contraband guns and ammunition and fashioned crude barricades, one for the male fighters, another for the women and children. The men let go a volley of shots as the small Confederate detachment approached. Their fire was answered, again and again. They were determined to fight to the death, expecting it to come soon. The women led the praying at their barricade. Only a few shells remained. Preacher Will, at the men's barricade, prayed more intensely for the Lord to help them:

"Lawd, you said when Zion cried, you was gwinter heah. Lawd, Zion is cryin' dis mawnin'. Lawd, buil' up Zion's wall. . . ."

The brave band could hardly believe their ears and eyes as, in the distance, the shrill notes of a bugle sounded. Immediately, the rain of shots against the barricade stopped. The Gray Coats were running as though pursued by demons. That night around the campfire, Preacher Will told the Federal soldiers, including the proud ex-slaves who had joined the Union army, of their experience in the swamp. Before they knew it, a song came forth: "Great day, great day, the righteous marchin', Great day, Gawd's gonna buil' up Zion's wall. . . ."

In the Bible, Zion refers to the church, the seat of God's rule. Jerusalem is its earthly capital and the symbol of the Kingdom of God. In songs such as "Great Day! Great Day!" from the later period of slavery, Zion signified also the New Jerusalem, the Kingdom of Heaven. Earlier, Zion had referred to Liberia or Ethiopia, anywhere in Africa, Africa itself being Zion. In the case of the early African-American believers, Zion depicted the slaves' resistance to their forced servitude. "Great Day! Great Day!" is no less defiant in its insistence that "We want no cowards in our band . . . We call for valiant-hearted men . . . Going to take my . . . sword and shield . . . And march out boldly in the field. . . ."

He Arose

Traditional Spiritual

1. They cru - ci - fied my Sav - ior   and nailed Him to the cross,   They

cru - ci - fied   my   Sav - ior   and   nailed Him to   the cross,

2. cross,— And the   Lord   will bear   my   spir - it   home.

He 'rose, He 'rose, He 'rose— from the dead, He
He 'rose, He 'rose,
'rose, He 'rose, He 'rose— from the dead,
He 'rose, He 'rose,
dead,— And the Lord— shall bear— my spir - it home.

2. *And Joseph begged His body and*
   laid it in the tomb,
   And Joseph begged His body and
   laid it in the tomb,
   And Joseph begged His body and
   laid it in the tomb,
   And the Lord will bear my spirit
   home.

3. *The cold grave could not hold Him*
   nor death's cold iron band,
   The cold grave could not hold Him
   nor death's cold iron band,

The cold grave could not hold Him
nor death's cold iron band,
And the Lord will bear my spirit
home.

4. *An Angel came from Heaven and*
   rolled the stone away,
   An Angel came from Heaven and
   rolled the stone away,
   An Angel came from Heaven and
   rolled the stone away,
   And the Lord will bear my spirit
   home.

5. *Sister Mary, she came running a-*
    looking for my Lord,
   Sister Mary, she came running a-
    looking for my Lord,
   Sister Mary, she came running a-
    looking for my Lord,
   And the Lord will bear my spirit
    home.

6. *The angel said He is not here,*
    He's gone to Galilee,
   The angel said He is not here,
    He's gone to Galilee,
   The angel said He is not here,
    He's gone to Galilee,
   And the Lord will bear my spirit
    home.

*A*n old spiritual shouts out, "God's not dead—He's alive!" In this song based on the Gospel of Matthew 28:1–5, the slaves, boasting in their Lord, sang contemptuously at those who crucified Him, who led Him away to be whipped, nailed, killed, and buried. They sang contemptuously because of His ultimate victory. The slaves were persuaded that the Lord's death brought them life—and life abundantly. Because Jesus arose from the dead, they were confident that He would also bear their spirits home to live eternally with Him.

This most joyous song brilliantly yet simply conveys its emotion in its words and melodic, rhythmic patterns. With its call-and-response style, the song accents—with the leader's "He 'rose" and the chorus's confirmation of "He 'rose"—the powerful message of Jesus' resurrection from the dead. It moves from the dark drama of the Crucifixion, often described in the spirituals, to the glorious certainty that "God's not dead—He's alive!"

This song tells of Jesus being buried in a borrowed grave belonging to the wealthy Joseph of Arimathea. It tells of an angel rolling back the stone from the door of the tomb. It also tells of Mary running excitedly from the tomb to tell Jesus' fearful, doubting disciples that He was not in the grave—"He is risen!"

Finally, as is characteristic in the spirituals, the song's authors bring the message back to their own circumstances, confident that their daily world is not the ultimate one for them. In the end, because of Jesus' sacrifice for them, they have the chance to triumph over evil. "The Lord will bear my spirit home," they sing, to live eternally with Him. That was the ultimate faith and hope that inspired this powerful spiritual—as well as so many others.

His Name So Sweet

Traditional Spiritual

Chorus

Oh, Lawd, I jes come from de foun-tain, I'm

jes from de foun-tain, Lawd,— Jes come from de foun-tain, His

1. name so sweet. Oh, Lawd, I **2.** name so sweet. *Fine*

Leader **Response**

1. Po' Sin-nuh, do you love Je-sus?— Yes, yes, I do love mah Je-sus.

Leader **Response** *D.C.*

Sin-nuh, do you love Je - sus?— His name so sweet.

2. *Class leader, do you love Jesus?*
   Yes, yes, I do love mah Jesus.
   Class leader, do you love Jesus?
   His name so sweet.

3. *'Sidin' elder, do you love Jesus?*
   Yes, yes, I do love mah Jesus.
   'Sidin' elder, do you love Jesus?
   His name so sweet.

4. *Brother, do you love Jesus?*
   Yes, yes, I do love mah Jesus.
   Brother, do you love Jesus?
   His name so sweet.

5. *Sister, do you love Jesus?*
   Yes, yes, I do love mah Jesus.
   Sister, do you love Jesus?
   His name so sweet.

*T*o enslaved Christians, Jesus was the fountain of life, from whom eternal life flowed abundantly upon their parched and weary souls. They knew that the gospel of Jesus Christ was for those of every race and condition. Calling on His name through the nights of prayer and praise services, when they were touched by God's Spirit, these believers found refreshment and strength for the days ahead. Here again we find an example of how integral to the spirituals biblical images and truths are. In the story of the woman at the well, in John 4:7–26, Jesus tells this despised and sinful outcast of Jewish society—a prostitute, a Samaritan—what He had not told others: "I am the Messiah!" The woman had been startled that a Jewish man would talk to her at all in a public place. But Jesus gave her "an extraordinary message about fresh and pure water that would quench her spiritual thirst forever," water that would become a perpetual spring within, watering her with eternal life. Jesus broke all the rules of the establishment in talking to this woman who was considered an outcast, an "untouchable" of society. For those who could so easily relate to her status, this story was especially meaningful.

The fountain appears as a symbol in the Bible in other ways as well. It refers to the Spirit of God dwelling inside believers. Devout Christians looked forward to the "crystal fountains" on the Great Day of deliverance when they would stand, worshipping God, in the throne room of Heaven. The flowing of the blood of Jesus on the Cross of Calvary, as in the hymn "There Is a Fountain," is also associated with this symbol.

"His Name So Sweet" is built on all of these references. It is also a testimony song and one of exhortation. With humor, the believer is checking on possible hypocrites, shaking his finger at the "poor sinnuh" and others who should be walking right, staying on the path. "Do you love Jesus?" the song asks the Methodist class leader. This class leader looked after small groups of congregation members, meeting with them during the week for Bible study (circumstances and slave holders permitting), praying, testifying, and singing. The song also speaks to the presiding elder—just because you preach doesn't mean you're really a Christian, the song challenges. The elder was an itinerant Methodist supervisor of congregations on plantations (slaves were allowed by some slave masters to travel for this purpose). The 'sidin' (presiding) elder was sometimes called "slidin' elder" if he came across as being less than devout or sincere, or appeared to be a backslider. Pious Christians in the slave community had low tolerance for hypocrites, whether they had titles, were backbiting, scandalizing brothers or sisters, or were rank sinners pretending to the faith.

Hold On

Traditional Spiritual

2. *Nora said, "Ya lost yo' track,*
   Can' plow straight an' keep
   a-lookin' back." . . .

3. *If you wanna get to Heaven, let me*
   tell you how:
   Just keep yo' han' on de gospel
   plow. . . .

4. *If dat plow stays in yo' han'*
   It'll lan' you straight into de
   promised lan'. . . .

5. *Mary had a golden chain.*
   Ev'ry link was my Jesus' name.

6. *Keep on climbin' an' don't you tire.*
   Ev'ry rung goes high'r an'
   high'r. . . .

*S*truggling with the tribulations and hardships of slave existence, believers needed the encouragement of others not to give up but to hold on. As a later gospel song says, "Hold to God's unchanging hand"—trust in His deliverance, keep pressing on. This exhortation is based on Luke 9:62, which says, "Anyone who puts a hand to the plow and then looks back is not fit for the Kingdom of God." Another scripture, 1 Corinthians 9:10, says that those who plow should do so in hope.

"Hold On" imaginatively uses its imagery to hearten, exhort, and teach the message of the scriptures. "Nora" is probably a mis-transcription of Noah (it also shows up in the printed version of the spiritual "Didn't It Rain," clearly the story of Noah). The sinner is asking to get into the ark—to be saved, in other words—but Noah admonishes that he is a backslider who has lost his track. He declares that, like Lot's wife, the sinner has looked back when going forward on the path to deliverance, which was the only way to the Promised Land. The song's chorus talks to the whole slave community, from brothers and mothers to deacons and preachers. All must watch their step and hold on to the great gospel plow. The plow and track are interesting images because they relate not only to the scriptural passages at the heart of "Hold On," but also to ordinary, everyday activities.

Another song of exhortation that was often sung one to another was, "Hold on, don't turn back, don't make my Leader [Jesus] 'shamed. Mistreated sometimes, don't turn back, don't make my Leader 'shamed." The underlying theme among the slaves, in spite of their dire, seemingly hopeless situation, was to "hold on," never to give up or let go of the plow, keep pressing on, and trust in God's deliverance, which they believed was sure to come.

I Know It Was the Blood

Traditional Spiritual

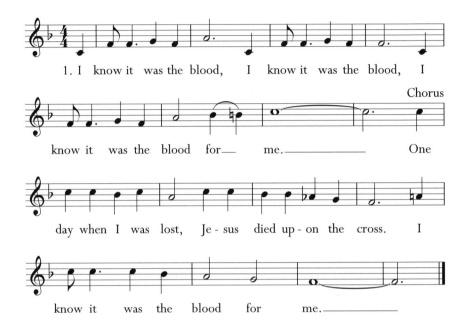

1. I know it was the blood, I know it was the blood, I know it was the blood for me.

Chorus

One day when I was lost, Je-sus died up-on the cross. I know it was the blood for me.

2. *It was my Savior's blood,*
   It was my Savior's blood,
   It was my Savior's blood for me.

3. *The blood came streaming down,*
   The blood came streaming down,
   The blood came streaming down
      for me.

4. *He suffered, bled, and died,*
   He suffered, bled, and died,
   He suffered, bled, and died for me.

5. *I know He's coming back,*
   I know He's coming back,
   I know He's coming back for me.

*T*alk of the blood, to those who are not familiar with its meaning, is un-pleasant, to say the least. And yet the symbol of blood is a very powerful one for Christians. It had especially powerful meaning to the early African-American believers. In this simple song, the slave testifies to the power of the blood of the Lamb—Jesus—that saves, forgives, cleanses, sanctifies. The Bible states that without the shedding of blood—specifically Christ's blood—

there is no remission (or forgiveness) of sins; that without His death there is no deliverance. It is from these beliefs that the songwriters declared, "I know it was the blood for me." The slave preaches in just a few words the message of redemption and salvation through Jesus Christ: His suffering, bleeding, death, and soon-coming return to take his people home to Heaven. The strong imagery and subject matter are another example of the deep identification the song's authors felt with the death and resurrection of Jesus.

This song is still sung frequently in the African-American church, especially after communion. It is a rejoicing, praising, dancing, shouting song of victory. It exemplifies the Christian tradition of celebrating the Last Supper, a tradition established by Jesus and the disciples when they left the Upper Room after sharing the wine and bread together. The Bible teaches that when Jesus was on His way to the cross, He and the disciples went out from the Upper Room singing a hymn.

Another hymn sung very often in the black church says, "Redeemed, redeemed, redeemed by the Blood of the Lamb! Redeemed, redeemed, His child, and forever I am!" The contemporary African-American composer and arranger Andrae Crouch has written a wonderful song of praise testifying to the power of the blood of Jesus in the believer's life, "The Blood Will Never Lose Its Power." This song is found in the final section of this book on the contemporary gospel songs.

The early African-American Christians had a deep understanding of the importance of these songs about the blood of Jesus. Their declarations of these truths through music not only sustained them, but brought them from the place of feeling like victims to being victors.

I Want Jesus to Walk with Me

Traditional Spiritual

Chorus

I want Je - sus   to walk with me, I want Je - sus   to walk with me,   All a - long my   pil - grim jour - ney,   I   want Je - sus   to walk with me.

1. In my tri - als,   Lord walk with me, In my

tri - als, — Lord walk with me, When the shades of — life — are

fall - ing, — Lord, I want Je - sus — to walk with me.

2. *In my sorrows, Lord walk with me,*
   In my sorrows, Lord walk with me,
   When my heart within is aching,
   Lord, I want Jesus to walk with me.

3. *In my troubles, Lord walk with me,*
   In my troubles, Lord walk with me,
   When my life becomes a burden,
   Lord, I want Jesus to walk with me.

*E*dward H. Boatner, an African-American singer, composer, and arranger, born in 1898 in New Orleans, was one of the leading authorities on the spiritual. He scored a most dramatic piano arrangement of "I Want Jesus to Walk with Me," which became one of his best-known pieces. Boatner used a rhythmic pattern that musically evokes one's footsteps on the long journey of life, through the trials, sorrows, and troubles this song so poignantly suggests. The enslaved song creators' longing for comfort in Jesus is so vividly presented and so deeply affecting that this song remains a favorite for choral and solo performances.

Boatner, whose spiritual arrangements were widely sung, was most responsible, along with composer-arrangers Harry T. Burleigh, R. Nathaniel Dett, and Hall Johnson, for developing the spiritual for the denomination/

mainline church and concert stage. He was a deeply religious man who began collecting spirituals at an early age. In addition to arranging spirituals, Boatner also wrote in some of the larger musical forms, with works including *Freedom Suite* and *The Man from Nazareth,* a "spiritual musical."

African-American Christians found great comfort and encouragement in believing that this life was only a journey—a "passing through"—to a better place. Although they hoped and prayed for deliverance and freedom in this life, they were fully convinced they would receive it in the life to come. As they passed through the bitter trials on this earth, their desire was that they not walk alone, but that Jesus walk with them. Knowing that Jesus, who had already passed through the fiery trials and come out triumphant on the other side, was walking beside them gave them courage to go on.

I Want to Be Ready (Walk in Jerusalem)

Traditional Spiritual

1. John said the cit-y was just four-square, Walk in Je-ru-sa-lem just like John. And
he de-clared he'd meet me there, Walk in Je-ru-sa-lem just like John.

2. *O John, O John, what do you say?*
   Walk in Jerusalem just like John.
   That I'll be there at the coming day,
   Walk in Jerusalem just like John.

3. *When Peter was preaching at*
   Pentecost,
   Walk in Jerusalem just like John.

He was endowed with the Holy
Ghost,
Walk in Jerusalem just like John.

4. *If you get there before I do,*
   Walk in Jerusalem just like John.
   Tell all my friends I'm-a comin' too,
   (Tell my mother . . .)
   (Tell my father . . .)
   Walk in Jerusalem just like John.

While unfailingly seeking freedom here on earth, Christian African-Americans in slavery never stopped looking forward to being forever free, going on to Heaven to walk the streets of gold. This song, in the camp-meeting, call-and-response style, expresses this joy and certainty. "I Want to Be Ready" has an additional verse, among those so-called traveling or floating verses because they moved from song to song. This verse adds to the overall picture painted by the song:

Some came crippled, some came lame,
Walk in Jerusalem just like John.
Some came walkin' in Jesus' name,
Walk in Jerusalem just like John.

Devout believers wanted to take care that they would be prepared when the Lord came for them, so they were "readying their white robes" (symbolic of righteousness). They dreamed of the time when they would walk around Heaven with Peter and John, and sit down at the banqueting table with Mark and Timothy. They revered these men of God, yet they had a lovingly familiar attitude toward the saints who had gone before. This was especially true in the cases of the apostles and disciples of Jesus—another example of the way African-Americans experienced their faith in a uniquely direct and personal way.

These enslaved men and women, in such a lowly position here on earth, believed that with those men of God they shared in the inheritance of eternal life. They looked forward with longing and excitement to the time when they would walk all over God's Heaven "just like John." The City of Heaven—New Jerusalem—is what the apostle John speaks of in the Book of Revelation. Although in slavery, often brutally torn from loved ones, these African-Americans were confident that they would be reunited with their dear ones in Heaven.

Slave letters and narratives of the eighteenth and nineteenth centuries abundantly attest to such feelings. An example is George Pleasant, writing in September 1833 from Shelbyville, Tennessee, to his wife, Agnes Hobbs, in Virginia. He writes that he hopes "with Gods helpe that I may be abble to rejoys with you on the earth and In Heaven lets meet . . . I am determnid to nuver stope praying, . . . In glory there weel meet to part no more forever. So my dear wife I hope to meet you In paradase to prase God forever. . . ." He adds poignantly, "I want Elizabeth to be a good girl and not thinke that because I am bound so fare [enslaved in a faraway state] that Gods not abble to open the way."

In Dat Great Gittin' Up Mornin'

Traditional Spiritual

Intro

I'm a goin' to tell you 'bout de com-in' of the Sav - ior,

1.
Fare you well, Fare you well;

2.
Fare you well, Fare you well.

Verses

1. {Dere's a bet-ter day a-com-in' } Fare you well, Fare you well;
{Pray - er mak-er, pray no— mo', }

{O preach-er, fol' yo' Bi-ble, } Fare you well, Fare you well.
{For the las' soul's con-vert-ed, }

Chorus

In dat great git-tin' up morn-in', Fare you well, Fare you well;

(to next verse)

In dat great git-tin' up morn-in', Fare you well, Fare you well.

2. Dat de time shall be no longer, . . .
   For judgment day is comin', . . .
   Den you hear de sinner sayin' . . .
   Down I'm rollin' down I'm
     rollin', . . .

3. De Lord spoke to Gabriel, . . .
   Go look behin' de altar, . . .
   Take down de silvah trumpet, . . .
   Blow yo' trumpet Gabriel; . . .

4. Lord how loud shall I blow it, . . .
   Blow it right calm an' easy, . . .
   Do not alarm my people, . . .
   Tell 'em to come to judgment; . . .

5. Gabriel blow yo' trumpet, . . .
   Lord, how loud shall I blow it, . . .
   Loud as seven peals of thunder, . . .
   Wake de livin' nations, . . .

6. Place one foot upon de dry
     lan', . . .
   Place de other on de sea, . . .

   Den you'll see de coffins
     bustin', . . .
   See de dry bones come a-
     creepin', . . .

7. Hell shall be uncapp'd an'
     burnin', . . .
   Den de dragon shall be
     loosen'd, . . .
   Where you runnin' po' sinner, . . .
   Where you runnin' po' sinner, . . .

8. Den you'll see po' sinners
     risin', . . .
   Den you'll see de worl' on
     fiah, . . .
   See de moon a bleedin', . . .
   See de stars a fallin', . . .

9. See de elements a meltin', . . .
   See de forked lightnin', . . .
   Den you'll cry out for cold
     water, . . .
   While de Christians shout in
     glory, . . .

10. *Sayin' Amen to yo'*
    damnation, . . .
    No mercy for po' sinner, . . .
    Hear de rumblin' of de
    thunder, . . .
    Earth shall reel an' totter, . . .

11. *Den you'll see de Christian*
    risin', . . .
    Den you'll see de righteous
    marchin', . . .

See dem marchin' home to
Heab'n, . . .
Den you'll see my Jesus comin', . . .

12. *Wid all His holy angels, . . .*
    Take de righteous home to
    glory, . . .
    Dere dey live wid God forever, . . .
    On de right hand side of my
    Saviour, . . .

*A*n early collection of spirituals from 1887 calls this song "a remarkable paraphrase of a portion of the Book of Revelation, and one of the finest specimens of negro 'Spirituals.'" The collection brought together arrangements of choruses from African-American colleges. Two of those colleges were Fisk and Hampton, which formed groups both to preserve the music born during slavery and to raise funds for their fledgling institutions. The student who brought "In Dat Great Gittin' Up Mornin'" to the collectors was the soloist, and he gave them all that he could remember of the numerous verses. He commented that he had sometimes heard them sung for half an hour at a time by slaves in their midnight meetings in the woods.

In this case the actual origin of the song is told by the student singer. It seems he first heard his uncle sing the hymn, and his uncle then told him how it came about. There was an old slave who could neither read nor write. In fact, he couldn't even count the number of rails that he was required to split by his master, which was 150 a day. In spite of his illiteracy, he did his best to lead a Christian life. He looked forward to the final day of judgment, and often told his fellow servants about it. In the telling, he would sometimes make up a tune to go with the words, and then sing it in his cabin meetings.

This old man might have played the role of the so-called exhorter in African-American worship services. Usually a pious person who may not have been able to read or write, he (or she) would have a repertoire of spirituals that he could sing by heart. As song leader, he would teach the congregation by "lining out" the song. In this call-and-response style, the verses of "In Dat Great Gittin' Up Mornin'" would be the call, and the line "Fare you well, Fare you well" the response. Some of the essential functions of the spirituals were to exhort, encourage, and teach through song. This extraordinarily dramatic one, given to us through an illiterate old man, is an exceptional gift.

My Lord, What a Morning

Traditional Spiritual

Chorus

My Lord, what a morn-ing, My Lord, what a morn-ing,

My Lord, what a morn-ing, When the stars be-gin to fall.

Fine

Leader

You'll—hear the trum-pet sound to wake the na-tions un-der-ground,

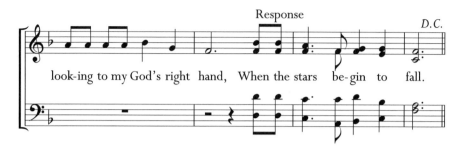

2. *You'll hear the sinner mourn,*
   To wake the nations underground,
   Looking to my God's right hand,
   When the stars begin to fall.

3. *You'll hear the Christian shout,*
   To wake the nations underground,
   Looking to my God's right hand,
   When the stars begin to fall.

(Verse from H. T. Burleigh arrangements):

4. *Done quit all my worl'ly ways,*
   Jine dat hebbenly ban?
   Done quit all my worl'ly ways,
   Jine dat hebbenly ban.

*W*hen enslaved worshippers were caught up in the intensity of communion with the Holy Spirit and with one another during their "hush harbor" prayer meetings, a new tune would often arise as a result. Hymns, Bible verses, sermons, and prayers were frequently the source of images and meanings. In the case of this spiritual, the inspiration seems to have been the hymn "Behold the Awful Trumpet Sounds." This hymn was first published in the 1801 hymnal of Richard Allen, the Philadelphia founder of the first independent black denomination, the African Methodist Episcopal (A.M.E.) Church. The words paint a vivid picture:

> *Behold the awful trumpet sounds,*
> *The sleeping dead to raise,*
> *And calls the nations underground:*
> *O how the saints will praise! . . .*
> *The falling stars their orbits leave,*
> *The sun in darkness hide:*
> *The elements asunder cleave,*
> *The moon turn'd into blood! . . .*

Some of the most striking spirituals are those that express the slaves' visions of the future, always in sharp contrast to their present conditions. These songs describe dramatically and in great detail the Day of Judgment. The despised slave was certain that morning, significant to the Christian as the time of deliverance, would bring the day of redemption and of ultimate victory. Then, at last, justice and right would triumph over evil.

On the morning "when the stars begin to fall," the song creators knew from the Bible, the trumpet will sound, heralding the Second Coming of Christ. Angels will blow the trumpet seven times during the time of divine judgments preceding His coming. Sinners, devastated, will mourn and tremble, while the Christian will shout and rejoice. It is this event that songs like "My Lord, What a Morning" and "In Dat Great Gittin' Up Mornin'" celebrate.

Nobody Knows de Trouble I've Seen

Traditional Spiritual

Chorus

No-bod-y knows de trou-ble I've seen, No-bod-y knows but Je-sus.

No-bod-y knows de trou-ble I've seen, Glo-ry Hal-le - lu-jah!

Fine

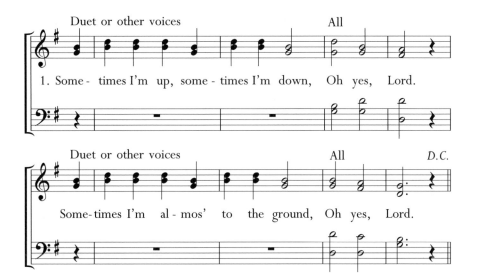

Duet or other voices   All

1. Some - times I'm up, some - times I'm down,   Oh yes,   Lord.

Duet or other voices   All   D.C.

Some - times I'm al - mos' to the ground,   Oh yes,   Lord.

2. *Although you see me goin' 'long so,*
   Oh yes, Lord.
   I have my trials here below,
   Oh yes, Lord.

3. *If you get there before I do,*
   Oh yes, Lord.
   Tell all-a my friends I'm coming too,
   Oh yes, Lord.

*T*his particular spiritual is one of the type sometimes referred to as a "sorrow song," and it is easy to see why. And yet, even in sorrow, the song points us to victory. "Glory Hallelujah!" the song declares, focusing on a joyous homecoming, rather than on the trials of this earthly life. Still, the powerful imagery of this song is a haunting reminder to all of us of the singularity of the slavery experience. African-Americans could reach only for the Sovereign God to comprehend that experience and to offer comfort in it. They found it in Jesus.

A story associates this song with a mother witnessing her daughter being sold away to another slaver, of her mourning not only the separation but the anguish and grief she hears in the cries of her child. Others outside the slave community were also deeply affected by the song. According to a contemporary report, General Oliver O. Howard, commissioner of the Freedmen's Bureau, which was formed following the Civil War to assist those coming out of slavery, was called upon to address some former slaves. This was at a time when there were a lot of ill feelings still unre-solved as a result of the war. Uncertainty about the government's actions regarding the confiscated lands formerly held by Southern plantation own-ers only added fuel to the flames of apprehension and anxiety. In this set-ting, Howard stood, about to address a meeting in the Sea Islands of South Carolina. However, he had a hard time maintaining his composure when an old woman and then the whole audience began to sing this song, an area favorite.

A formerly enslaved woman named Mrs. Brown, of Nashville, gave this song to collectors of jubilee and plantation songs for an 1887 book. She told them that she first heard it from her father when she was a child. After he had been whipped (an all too common, brutal practice), he always sat on a certain log near his cabin. With tears streaming down his cheeks, he sang the song with so much pathos that few listening could keep from weeping. It is reported that even those who participated in his beating were touched.

The intrinsic poetry of "Nobody Knows de Trouble I've Seen" pairs with the soulful music to achieve the song's deeply moving effect. The slow, sustained, long-phrase melody of the chorus contrasts just enough with the picked-up tempo of the verse to get across the sense of despair conquered by hope and faith in the Lord and by ultimate deliverance.

Oh, Freedom

Traditional Spiritual

And be - fore I'd be a slave, I'll be bur-ied in my

grave, And go home to my Lord and be free.

2. *No more moaning,*
   No more moaning,
   No more moaning over me!

3. *There'll be singing,*
   There'll be singing,
   There'll be singing over me!

4. *There'll be shouting,*
   There'll be shouting,
   There'll be shouting over me!

5. *There'll be praying,*
   There'll be praying,
   There'll be praying over me!

*W*hat a many-layered song this is! "Oh, Freedom" expresses longing for ultimate spiritual deliverance in death, beyond human concerns, when those still here will be singing, shouting, and praying over the believer, who will be home—free—with the Lord. But it also claims for those in the bondage of slavery their rightful inheritance of earthly freedom. In this context it was sometimes used as a message song about fleeing from slavery. In an almost overtly political way, it expresses a defiant mind-set, as stated in the chorus: "Before I'd be a slave, I'll be buried in my grave." The enslaved men and women did not accept slavery in their minds and hearts. They were able to elevate themselves above their circumstances and live victoriously with a bright future in view.

"Oh, Freedom" functioned on all of these levels to help African-Americans hold on to their humanity. A hundred years after slavery ended, the descendants of these men and women reached back and claimed the song for the same purpose in the continuing struggle to transform their hard-won homeland. It became one of the theme songs of the 1960s civil rights movement, its choruses resounding as African-Americans and their allies courageously battled the modern remnants of slavocracy. The spiritual form easily lent itself to this sort of use, and also to spontaneous and situational creation of lyrics. In the segregated and racially hostile South, instances such as a Sunday morning bombing of a church in which Sunday school children were killed or confrontations between marchers and officials using dogs or fire hoses, as in the confrontation with Police Chief Bull Connor in Birmingham, Alabama, in 1963, inspired these spontaneous lyrics. The movement often interspersed this song with contemporary verses appropriate to the situation:

> *Don' let nobody turn you aroun',*
> *Turn you aroun', turn you aroun',*
> *Don' let nobody turn you aroun',*
> *Walking up the King's Highway.*
>
> *Don' let segregation turn you aroun', . . .*
>
> *Don' let Bull Connor turn you aroun', . . .*
>
> *Don' let no jailhouse turn you aroun', . . .*

Today "Oh, Freedom" is used again in many churches in its original form and style. Most recently I heard the Male Chorus of about fifty men at the Allen A.M.E. Church sing this with strong and sonorous tenor and bass voices, and it was just as inspiring as it has ever been!

Oh! What a Beautiful City

Traditional Spiritual

Oh! What a beau-ti-ful cit-y,   Oh! What a beau-ti-ful cit-y,

Oh! What a beau-ti-ful cit-y, Twelve gates-a to the cit-y, Hal - le - lu!

1. Three gates in - a de east, Three gates in - a de west,

Three gates in - a de north, Three gates in - a de

D.C.

south, Mak-ing it twelve gates - a to de cit-y, Hal - le - lu!

2. *My Lord built-a dat city,*
   Said it was just-a fo' square;
   Wanted all-a you sinners
   To meet Him in-a de air;
   'Cause He built twelve gates-a to
      the city,
   Hallelu!

3. *Who are all-a those children*
   All dressed up in white?
   They must be the children
   Of the Israelites.
   'Cause He built twelve gates-a to
      the city,
   Hallelu!

4. *Who are all-a those children*
   All dressed up in red?
   They must be the children
   That Moses led.
   The Lord built twelve gates-a to
      the city,
   Hallelu!

5. *When I get to Heaven*
   I'm gonna sing and shout.
   Ain't nobody up there
   Gonna take me out.
   'Cause He built twelve gates-a to
      the city,
   Hallelu!

*A*frican-American preaching is probably the most dynamic in Christendom. The slave preacher in the hush harbors and praise houses of the invisible church was the forefather of the powerful black preaching tradition. The colorful visions of Heaven that are found in the spirituals come from his ability to bring the Bible to life. His teachings about Heaven probably included the beautiful city that the apostle John saw on the Isle of Patmos, described in the Book of Revelation, as well as the fact that in Heaven there would be no more tears, sorrow, or death. The slaves considered Heaven their home, that glorious place where all that was needed and desired would be found in the presence of Jesus. Envisioning the beauty and riches of that home was undoubtedly comforting to a people who had been ripped from their original home and treated like unwelcome strangers in their present one.

Again, in this song it is easy to see the enslaved relating to the Old Testament story of the freeing of the Israelite slaves. The blood of the sacrificial lambs was sprinkled over the doorposts of the Jews who had been held in Egypt by Pharaoh, and the exodus to the Promised Land began. Rejoicing, singing, shouting, with hallelujahs ringing in their hearts, the song authors were sure that, once they escaped this earth for the Promised Land, "Ain't nobody up there gonna take me out."

This faith sustained them through the many tragedies of slavery, especially the terrible enforced separation of families. In September 1835, Phebe Brownrigg wrote from Edenton, North Carolina, to her daughter, Amy: "My dear daughter, I have for some time had hope of seeing you once more in this world, but now that hope is entirely gone forever . . . if we never meet in this world, I hope we shall meet in Heaven. . . . Farewell, my dear child. I hope the Lord will bless you and your children, and enable you to raise them and be comfortable in life, happy in death, and may we all meet around our Father's throne in Heaven, never no more to part."

Ride On, King Jesus

Traditional Spiritual

Chorus

Ride on, King— Je - sus, No man can a - hin-der me,

Fine

Ride on, King— Je-sus, ride—on, No man—— can a - hin-der me.

1. I was but young when I be-gun, No man can a-hin-der me;

But now my race is al-most done,— No man— can a-hin-der me.

2. *King Jesus rides on a milk-white*
   horse,
   No man can a-hinder me;
   The river of Jordan he did cross,
   No man can a-hinder me.

3. *If you want to find your way to*
   God,
   No man can a-hinder me;
   The gospel highway must be trod,
   No man can a-hinder me.

4. *When I get to Heaven gonna wear*
   a robe,
   No man can a-hinder me;
   Gonna see King Jesus sittin' on the
   throne,
   No man can a-hinder me.

5. *Gonna walk all over those streets*
   of gold,
   No man can a-hinder me;
   Goin' to a land where I'll never
   grow old,
   No man can a-hinder me.

*I*t is not surprising that a people in slavery would need and prefer to relate to a mighty God. Picturing their chosen King, riding up majestically and triumphantly on a horse, inspired confidence and courage in their hearts. Quoting from the Scriptures, they undoubtedly asked themselves, "If God is for us, who can be against us?" Disenfranchised African-Americans sought and found their real leader above the human beings they had to contend with. Their arch-enemies—the devil on one hand, the slave master on the other—were no match for the God who was on their side. All the armies of opposition and oppression, General Robert E. Lee's Confederates among them, were no match for King Jesus. Sooner or later, they knew, He would conquer the slave system. The so-called meek rejoiced in singing fighting songs like "Ride On, King Jesus," "The Lord Is a Man of

War," "The Captain of the Army," "The Lord of Hosts," and "The King of Glory."

Some later arrangements of "Ride On, King Jesus" add the phrasing "He is the King of Kings, He is the Lord of Lords, Jesus Christ, the First and Last, no man hinders me!" The song is another example of the vivid depictions of Heaven the spirituals contain: Wearing the robes of righteousness, the believer will see King Jesus on the throne, walk the streets of gold, never grow old. But the song's second and third verses are probably speaking on more than the sacred level. They most likely contain coded messages about the Underground Railroad escape network, referring to a horse, a river, a certain road that must be used.

With that double meaning in mind, it is easy to see that this particular spiritual is actually a battle cry as well as a song of praise.

Sinner, Please Don't Let Dis Harves' Pass

Traditional Spiritual

Bro-ther, be sure— you got yo' soul right,   Sis-ter, be sure— you got yo'
heart right,   See de time— is wind-ing up,   Don't

please   don't let dis har-ves' pass,   Sin-ner,

pass,   Sin-ner, please don't let dis har-ves'

please   don't let   dis har - ves'   pass,   An'

pass,   Don't   let   dis har-ves' pass,

1., 2.   3.

die,   an' lose yo' soul at las'.——— 2. Sin-ner, see, —
                                    3. Broth - er, please,

An' die, an' lose yo' soul at las'.———

4. My God, He's a migh-ty man o' war,———————

(verse 5 on repeat)

My God,— He's a migh-ty man o'

My God, He's a migh-ty man o' war,———————

war, My God,— He's a migh-ty man o'

My God, He's a migh - ty man o' war,——— Sin-ner,

My God, He's a man o' war,

trust Him.

trust Him. Sin- ner, please don't

7. My Je- sus, He's a

let dis har - ves' pass.

rock in a wea - ry land,

He's a rock in a wea - ry land, He's a rock in a

please   don't   let dis har - ves' pass.

Sin- ner, please don't   let dis har - ves'   pass.

2. Sinner, see, O, see dat cruel tree,
   Sinner, see, O, see dat cruel tree,
   Sinner, see, O, see dat cruel tree,
   Where Christ has died for you
      an' me.

3. Brother, please, don't let de sun
      go down,
   Sister, please, don't let de sun
      go down,
   Brother, please, don't let de sun
      go down,
   An' die, an' lose yo' starry crown.

5. I know dat my Redeemer lives,
   I know dat my Redeemer lives,
   I know dat my Redeemer lives,
   Sinner, please don't let dis harves'
      pass.

6. I know dat my God,
   He will save you,
   If you trust Him.
   Sinner, please don't let dis harves'
      pass.

*C*an't you just hear the zealous believer pleading with his neighbor in the field or on the campground: "Come to Jesus! Don't let this harvest season go by without giving your life over to the Lord." Spreading the good news that our Redeemer lives, that Christ "died for you an' me, for you an' me, Lord," that He is a "mighty man o' war," and "a rock in a weary land" was a fervent mission for the enslaved Christian. For the early African-American, Jesus was indeed "a shelter in a time of storm."

I am reminded of another song by Ira D. Sankey (1840–1908), the well-known camp meeting–era evangelist and gospel writer, who wrote a melody to verses by Vernon J. Charlesworth, born in 1838.

The Lord's our Rock, in Him we hide,
A shelter in the time of storm,
Secure whatever ill be-tide,
A shelter in the time of storm. . . .

O Rock divine, O Refuge dear, . . .

O Jesus is a Rock in a weary land, a weary land,
O Jesus is a Rock in a weary land,
A shelter in a time of storm.

Twentieth-century composers have arranged many spirituals in contemporary musical settings. The dramatic "Sinner, Please Don't Let Dis
Harves' Pass" was set to an exciting gospel score by the Reverend Clinton
Utterbach, African-American pastor of Redeeming Love Christian Center
in Nanuet, New York. His arrangement is a popular number with choirs.
Reverend Utterbach, a gifted singer, composer, arranger, choral director,
and musician, was an important pioneer in the gospel arena. He was one of
the first to wed European classical discipline and technique to the vitality and
spirit of gospel, much as composer-arranger R. Nathaniel Dett did with the
spiritual.

Steal Away

Traditional Spiritual

Steal a-way, steal a-way, steal a-way to Je-sus!

Steal a-way, steal a-way home, I ain't got long to stay here!

1. My Lord, He calls me, He calls me by the thun-der; The

trum-pet sounds with-in-a my soul; I ain't got long to stay here!

2. Green trees a-bending,
   Poor sinner stands a-trembling:
   The trumpet sounds within-a my
      soul;
   I ain't got long to stay here!

3. My Lord, He calls me;
   He calls me by the lightning;
   The trumpet sounds within-a my
      soul;
   I ain't got long to stay here!

*I*n its brief verses, "Steal Away" spoke to the slave community with resonance. While the slave masters' preachers most often limited their sermons to the propaganda that sustained slavocracy, the slaves stole themselves and their spirits away to their secret hush harbors or even to freedom in the North via the Underground Railroad. "When [we] go round singin' 'Steal Away to Jesus,'" recalled one slave named Wash Wilson, "dat mean dere gwine be 'ligious meetin' dat night." The first phrase of the song would be hummed by a leader to another person who would hum the phrase in turn to someone else. The signal would be softly given all day until everyone was notified, and the slave master would never know what was going on. "De masters . . . didn't like dem 'ligious meetin's, so us natcherly slips off at night, down in de bottoms or somewhere. Sometimes us sing and also pray all night," Wilson added. Believers were also looking to steal away to be with Jesus in eternity.

It's clear from the testimony of fugitive and freed slaves that slave holders considered any evidence of an "invisible" church subversive or at least threatening. It's no wonder, since the songs and services were used in so many ways to communicate among the folk. Slave revolt leader Nat Turner, a preacher in Virginia, reportedly used this song to call his co-conspirators together. Slave holder responses to the discovery of services varied. Some might do no more than send someone to warn worshippers to stop the noise or else answer to abusive, violent patrollers. Others went so far as to flog the preacher "until his back pickled," then flog his listeners until they were forced to tell who else was there. An utmost punishment was meted out to a preacher in Georgia. This preacher, named George, disregarded his so-called master's threat of five hundred lashes if he continued preaching to his slave community. George escaped across the Savannah River to Greenville, South Carolina, in an attempt to avoid the whip. On the way, however, he ended up striking with a rifle a white man who had tried to shoot him. George was captured and jailed, and his master came to claim him, but was unable to do so. The authorities instead gave George's master $550 as payment for George's life. Then, in a wooden pen in front of a huge, forced assemblage of other enslaved African-Americans, Greenville officials burned George alive.

Sweet Jesus

Traditional Spiritual

1. Sweet Je - sus,— sweet Je - sus, He's the

Li - ly of the Val - ley, He's the Bright and Morn - ing Star. Sweet Je - sus, sweet Je - sus, He's the Fair - est of ten thou - sand to my soul.

2. *How I love Him, how I love Him,*
He's the Lily of the Valley,
He's the Bright and Morning Star.
How I love Him, how I love Him,
He's the fairest of ten thousand to
my soul.

3. *I'll serve Him, I'll serve Him,*
He's the Lily of the Valley,
He's the Bright and Morning Star.

I'll serve Him, I'll serve Him,
He's the fairest of ten thousand to
my soul.

4. *He's worthy, He's worthy,*
He's the Lily of the Valley,
He's the Bright and Morning Star.
He's worthy, He's worthy,
He's the governor of the nations,
bless His name.

*Y*ou can see throughout the African-Americans' sacred music that Jesus is adored, depended upon, experienced as a refuge, a solace, and a protector. Those early black Christians, under the yoke of slavery, were so deeply touched by Jesus, His suffering, His power, and His love that their lives and their songs became centered on Him. Not merely an adherence to a religious doctrine about God, their faith was personal, alive, vital—and, as in their African cultures, ever-present, unifying, and expressed in song. The Christianity of the slave community completely rejected the hypocritical religious practices and beliefs of slave holders and other apologists for slavery—and of anyone to whom the faith was merely conventional. There was a great difference between religion and Christianity, as South Carolina ex-slave Linda Brent, author of *Incidents in the Life of a Slave Girl,* stated. Or, as another former slave, Nancy Williams, put it: "That ol' white preachin' wasn't nothin' . . . Ol' white preacher used to talk with their tongues without saying nothin', but Jesus told us slaves to talk with our hearts."

"Sweet Jesus" is a heartfelt testament to their love for Him, their intimate friendship with Him. As in this song, such images of Jesus abound in the spirituals and throughout black sacred music. He is spoken of as honey to the lips, and referred to as the fairest of ten thousand. He is called the sweet Lily of the Valley of one's despair, the Bright and Morning Star in the darkness of one's existence. But those oppressed by slavery also esteemed Jesus in song as the Chiefest of All, worthy of honor and glory. He was the Mighty God, the Conquering King, the King of all nations. A frequently added "turnaround," "tag," or phrase to the last verse of "Sweet Jesus" underlines the conviction that Jesus was on their side:

> . . . *He's the governor of the nations,*
> *He's the King of all creation,*
> *He's the God of my salvation, yes He is.*

Swing Low, Sweet Chariot

Traditional Spiritual

Chorus

Swing low, sweet char - i - ot, — Com-ing for to car - ry me home,

Swing low, sweet char - i- ot, — Com-ing for to car-ry me home.

Fine

1. I looked o - ver Jor - dan, and what did I see, —

Com - ing for to car - ry me home? A band— of an - gels

com-ing af-ter me, — Com-ing for to car-ry me home.

D.C.

2. *If you get there before I do,*
   Coming for to carry me home,
   Tell all my friends I'm coming too,
   Coming for to carry me home.

3. *The brightest day that ever I saw,*
   Coming for to carry me home,
   When Jesus wash'd my sins away,
   Coming for to carry me home.

4. *I'm sometimes up, I'm sometimes*
   down,
   Coming for to carry me home,
   But still my soul feels heavenly
   bound,
   Coming for to carry me home.

*W*hat relief and expectation elderly or dying persons who had spent a lifetime under slavery must have felt as their time of deliverance drew near. The "sweet chariot" would soon take them "Heavenly bound." Over and over again in the spirituals the folk expressed reverent joy in going home to be with God, as well as the desire to be free from the literal and figurative chains of this world. Most of the biblical themes they chose as the basis of so many song texts were ones that showed God delivering the faithful from impossible circumstances by supernatural means. The story in 2 Kings of the prophet Elijah being caught up by God and whisked away in a chariot to Heaven may have been at least one of the biblical inspirations for this spiritual. These songs also borrowed from everyday images and folk beliefs to embellish their themes.

The "chariot" was a sled-like vehicle used by enslaved workers in the Carolinas to transport tobacco, according to author-playwright Vy Higginsen. Later, she explains, the chariot came to represent a way of escaping to freedom in Africa. It would "swing low" from the skies in order to fly the people away from America and back to the homeland. This theme of the power of flight, in its this-worldly and other-worldly aspects, is echoed in another spiritual:

Sometimes I feel like an eagle in de air,
Some-a dese mornin's bright an' fair
I'm goin' to lay down my heavy load,
Goin' to spread my wings an' cleave de air.

You may bury me in de east,
You may bury me in de west,
But I'll hear de trumpet sound
In-a dat mornin'.

The chorus and verses of "Swing Low, Sweet Chariot" are sung in the call-and-response style. That, combined with their multiple repetitions of "Coming for to carry me home," bring the song's multiple meanings and multilayered messages to an emotional pitch that was a comfort to singers and listeners alike.

Take Me to the Water

Traditional Spiritual

2. *None but the righteous,*
   None but the righteous,
   None but the righteous shall see
      God.

3. *I love Jesus,*
   I love Jesus,
   I love Jesus, yes I do.

4. *He's my Savior,*
   He's my Savior,
   He's my Savior, yes He is.

*W*ater baptism has always been a most treasured ceremony in the African-American church, and is greatly celebrated. The act of being baptized indicates that the participant, who has already repented (turned from sin to God) and acknowledged faith in Jesus, is making a full and public commitment to follow Christ and to submit to his Lordship. In many Baptist churches in the rural South, baptism is still carried out by the traditional method of total immersion. On Hilton Head Island, South Carolina, the Mount Calvary Baptist Church is famous for its services, which involve many days of preparation. Their baptismal services are so well-known that they have been featured in the area's major newspaper. Preceding a baptismal service, Mount Calvary's baptismal candidates and congregation can be seen going from the church on Squire Pope Road down Hudson Road to the river. They do so dressed in white from head to toe—an image that is as old as Christendom and an indelible part of the Southern landscape.

   There was a time in the South, in the early days of slavery under the British, when English planters thought baptism, according to their country's laws and church, made it necessary to free a slave—and so they forbade the ritual. This caused great problems for many of the missionaries and evangelists, who took biblical directives literally. The Bible states that people must be converted and baptized to be saved; Jesus also commanded His followers to "make disciples, baptizing them in my name." As a result of the controversy over baptizing slaves, by the early 1700s it became colonial law that baptism did not affect an Englishman's right to hold an African in perpetual bondage. Great numbers of Africans became Christians through the next century. As this happened, being baptized as an outward sign of an inward change (that of having been "saved" and "born again" in Christ) was one of the most meaningful and dramatic rituals for black believers, especially for Baptists or converts from revival meetings. The act of baptism symbolized the believer's union and identification with Christ in His death, burial, and resurrection. Here is the way ex-slave Isaiah Jeffries described it: "When I got to be a big boy, my Ma got religion at de Camp meeting at El-Bethel. She shouted and sung fer three days, going all over de plantation and de neighboring ones, inviting her friends to come to see her baptized and shouting and praying fer dem."

Many who lived on a Roman Catholic or Methodist plantation, like Elizabeth Ross Hite, were secret Baptists. "See, our master didn't like us to have too much 'ligion, said it made us lag in our work," Elizabeth recalled. "He jest wanted us to be Catholicses on Sunday . . . didn't want us shoutin' and moanin' all day long, but you gotta shout and moan if you wants to be saved."

There Is a Balm in Gilead

Traditional Spiritual

1. Some - times I feel dis - cour - aged, And think my work's in vain,

D.C.

But then the Ho - ly Spir - it Re - vives my soul a - gain._____

2. *Don't ever feel discouraged,*
   For Jesus is your friend,
   And if you lack for knowledge,
   He'll ne'er refuse to lend.

3. *If you cannot preach like Peter,*
   If you cannot pray like Paul,
   You can tell the love of Jesus,
   And say, "He died for all."

*G*ilead, located on the eastern shore of the Jordan River, was a lush and fra-grant area, abounding with wildflowers and beautiful forests and glens—in sharp contrast to the stark barrenness of the rest of Palestine. This district was widely known for its precious balm—a soothing, healing ointment—which had great medicinal and aromatic value. Its worth in silver was as priceless as salt in the ancient world. In a well-known Bible story, King David ran to Gilead when he fled from his traitorous son, Absalom, who was trying to take over the throne.

"Is there no balm in Gilead?" is the question the Old Testament prophet Jeremiah posed as he grieved over the sin of the Israelites who had turned their back on God and refused to repent. The enslaved African-Americans found in their new religion the answer, and they sang about it: "Yes, there is a balm in Gilead, To heal the sin-sick soul . . . To make the wounded whole." That balm was Jesus Christ. For the afflicted, bruised, and broken soul of the African-American under the horrendous oppression of slavery, the knowledge of Christ brought healing and deliverance.

The text of this still-popular song captures this soothing, timeless message. It says to the Christian: If you're discouraged, if you can't preach like the prophets of old, there is still something for you to do. You can testify to the love of Jesus for all—rich or poor, high or low, black or white, red or yellow.

In performance, the song's rich and comforting harmonies and melodic line and its lyrical cadences, along with its healing message, make "There Is a Balm in Gilead" a timeless, appealing favorite.

This Little Light of Mine

Traditional Spiritual

This lit- tle light of mine, — I'm going to let it shine, let it shine, let it shine, — let it shine. (let it shine)

2. *All in my heart, . . .*

3. *All in my house, . . .*

4. *Ev'rywhere I go, . . .*

5. *Out in the dark, . . .*

*T*his Little Light of Mine," known as a "testifying" song, expresses its authors' zealous and exuberant devotion to the Lord. It is based, as so many spirituals are, on solid biblical precepts and symbols. In this case, the suggested Scripture is from Matthew 5:14–16, when Jesus tells his disciples, "You are the world's light—a city on a hill, glowing in the night for all to see. Don't hide your light! Let it shine for all: let your good deeds glow for all to see, so that they will praise your Heavenly Father." Light also represents God and God's Word in Psalm 119:105: "Your word is a lamp for my feet and a light for my path." The New Testament presents Jesus as the personification of light or divine illumination in John 8:12: "I am the light of the world."

The liveliness of this song and its simple lyrics also make it appealing to children. It was especially a favorite when my daughter, Maya, was four years old and my son, Jimmy, was three. They had just received their first record player, a jazzy-looking bright yellow one. They played "This Little Light of Mine" over and over all day long, whether they were eating, playing, or even *supposed* to be sleeping. With great animation they sang along, particularly the verse that is often added to the song: "Hide it under a bushel? No! I'm gonna let it shine!"

Another dimension of this song is its appeal to the inner strength of its singers, its declaration of humanity held sacred under all conditions. When the great Mississippi civil rights leader Fannie Lou Hamer, a religious woman in touch with the old songs, lifted her voice in song frequently during the 1960s movement, this was one of her favorites. Mrs. Hamer and her Mississippi Freedom Democratic Party failed in their challenge to the seating of the state's racist, all-white delegation at the 1964 National Democratic Convention. But the full force of this song and its singers was memorably employed during at least one episode of that battle.

Wade in the Water

Traditional Spiritual

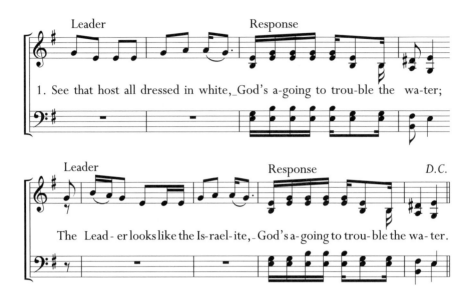

1. See that host all dressed in white, God's a-going to trouble the water;

The Leader looks like the Is-rael-ite, God's a-going to trouble the water.

2. See that band all dressed in red,
   God's a-going to trouble the water;
   Looks like the band that Moses led,
   God's a-going to trouble the water.

3. Look over yonder, what do I see?
   God's a-going to trouble the water;

The Holy Ghost a-coming on me,
   God's a-going to trouble the water.

4. If you don't believe I've been redeemed,
   God's a-going to trouble the water;
   Just follow me down to Jordan's stream,
   God's a-going to trouble the water.

*W*hen God "troubled," or moved, the water it was a sign that healing would take place. In the Gospel of John 5:1–9 a crippled man sat beside the pool of Bethesda for a long time, waiting for an angel to come and stir (or "trouble") the waters so that he could be dipped into the water and healed. As so often happened, when the angel came down there was no one around to pick the man up and place him in the water. But one day Jesus came by and touched the man and healed him.

Water is a common cleansing symbol in the spirituals. It refers most of the time to the redemptive power of the River Jordan. With great imaginative accuracy, the authors of "Wade in the Water" allude in the last verse to "Jordan's stream"—and the Jordan actually does start as a stream from a mountainside. By word-painting in deft strokes, the biblical account of Jesus' baptism in the Jordan by His cousin John the Baptist is also included: "The leader looks like the Israelite." Also, in the last two verses the narrator's own "quickening" or receiving of new life by the Holy Ghost during baptism is referred to, the occasion for him (or her) to publicly declare rebirth in Christ.

The "host all dressed in white" whose "leader looks like the Israelite" and the "band all dressed in red . . . that Moses led" are images used in "traveling," "wandering," or "floating" phrases or verses, which reappear consistently from song to song. These floating verses, for example, can be found in "Oh! What a Beautiful City," included earlier in this section.

"Wade in the Water" was a song used by Underground Railroad slave conductor Harriet Tubman to warn her fleeing charges how to throw pursuing bloodhounds off their scent.

Were You There?

Traditional Spiritual

1. Were you there when they cru - ci - fied my Lord? (were you there?)

Were you there when they cru - ci - fied my Lord? Oh!

Some-times it caus - es me to trem-ble, trem-ble, trem-ble,

Were you there when they cru - ci - fied my Lord?

2. *Were you there when they nailed*
   Him to the tree? . . .

3. *Were you there when they pierced*
   Him in the side? . . .

4. *Were you there when the sun*
   refused to shine? . . .

5. *Were you there when they laid*
   Him in the tomb? . . .

6. *Were you there when they rolled*
   the stone away? . . .

7. *Did you know He is risen from*
   the dead?
   Did you know He is risen from
   the dead?
   Oh! Sometimes I want to shout,
   "Glory, Glory, Glory!"
   Did you know He is risen from
   the dead?

*T*his passionate, dramatic retelling of the story of the death and resurrection of Jesus Christ is one of the finest in a group of unforgettable spirituals portraying the Crucifixion. The text is so powerful we do feel as if we were there. And the music deepens the feeling with slow, majestic, sustained phrasing. We are led step by terrible step through the agonizing ordeal of Christ's time on the cross "when the sun refused to shine." It is not surprising that people experiencing the tragedy of American slavery could identify so closely with the suffering of Christ. The spirituals return again and again to the haunting scenes of the Crucifixion. "Hammering,"

"He Arose," "They Led My Lord Away," and "He Never Said a Mumblin'
Word" are some of them. For example:

> *Dey crucified my Lord,*
> *An' He never said a mumblin' word.*
> *Dey crucified my Lord,*
> *An' He never said a mumblin' word,*
> *Not a word—not a word—not a word.*
>
> *Dey nailed Him to de tree, . . .*
>
> *Dey pierced Him in de side, . . .*
>
> *De blood came twinklin' [trickling] down, . . .*
>
> *He bowed His head an' died, . . .*

"Were You There?" brings home its graphic images so effectively also by
being doubly repetitive in melody and lyrics. It uses a pattern in its
melodic line that repeats with only slight variation (as in the first two lines
of the chorus and verses), and it repeats throughout the song in the lead
lyric line ("Were you there . . ."). When we listen to or sing this song, we
are there, trembling. Christ's brutal torture becomes tangible. His death
lies heavy, and we are grief-stricken.

The last stanza takes us from such trials to triumph. It may not ever
have been published, but it has been passed down through the oral tradition, and it completes the picture. For the song's creators, it was the ultimate victory that gave them hope for another, better life.

This song is especially meaningful to me. On Easter Sunday 1968, the
Sunday immediately following the assassination of Martin Luther King Jr.,
I sang it at the Community Church in mid-Manhattan, where a civil rights
advocate, the Reverend Donald Harrington, was pastor. As I sang this
heartfelt song, NBC-TV filmed the service, trying to capture the grief of
the nation in light of the shame of this incident. Martin Luther King Jr.
was truly a soldier of freedom, whose heart was to "set the captives free"
from poverty and injustice—regardless of race or social, cultural, or economic status.

II.

The Gospel Songs

Gospel Hymns, Historical Gospel, and Traditional Songs
Songs of Tindley, Dorsey, Campbell, and others,
1870–1960

We've come this far by faith
Leaning on the Lord;
Trusting in His Holy Word,
He's never failed me yet.
Oh, can't turn around,
We've come this far by faith.

*G*ospel music, with its soul-stirring tunes and melodies, as well as its lyrics that speak to us "where we are," attracts more people perhaps than any other type of music. It is used not only in African-American churches, but also in white churches and in gospel choirs within and outside the church. But it is important to note that there are some basic differences in the style, tone, and structure of gospel music as it is sung in different churches and by different gospel choirs.

Gospel music is more than a certain type of song. It is a feeling, or an expression of feelings, that releases its singers to "sing a new song" each time a song is performed, even while repeating the already familiar words. In addition, gospel music is spontaneous because it is inspired by the Holy Spirit. This type of spontaneous, personally expressed gospel singing is usually more prevalent in the black church than in the white.

Because there is no specific cutoff date for the waning of one style of music and the rise of another, you will find much overlapping in the four sections of this book. The influencing and blending of one musical style with the next makes specific dating of the eras of spirituals, hymns, or gospel music almost impossible. Due to that carryover influence, I have chosen to date this section on gospel hymns from 1870 to 1960, although we will be concentrating primarily on songs written from the late 1920s to the 1950s. First, though, let me bring you up to date.

Following the Civil War and Emancipation, the 1870s were the era of Reconstruction. Approximately four million slaves had been set free, and government and social agencies, including the Freedmen's Bureau, were established to help them in the transition. But little was accomplished in the way of actual assistance. Other than being legally declared free, many of the former slaves were no better off than they had been prior to the Civil War.

Although the majority of the newly freed slaves remained in the South, large numbers of them began a northward migration. With dreams of employment and opportunity beckoning them, African-Americans soon found themselves in yet another strange land, the North, the home of the Unionists who had helped fight for the slaves' freedom. Sadly, most did not find the welcome they had hoped for. Although some were able to find and maintain employment, the competition with whites seeking employment in a white-owned business and industrial world was formidable. Prejudice and racism may have been a bit more subtle than in the South, but they were still very real factors.

With this migration to the North came the urbanization of African-Americans, as they moved from the country to the cities in search of employment and housing. And when the blacks moved in, the whites moved out. It was obvious that although the slaves had been emancipated, they were still disenfranchised. It was in this setting that the seeds of gospel music began to grow.

There are two main divisions of gospel music: historic gospel, which began as early as 1870 but is usually considered to span from the years just prior to the depression up to the 1950s; and contemporary or modern gospel, which includes gospel songs written from the 1960s to the present. Although the civil rights movement wasn't in full swing until the beginning of the contemporary gospel era, it had already begun during the end of the historic gospel period, producing what are sometimes referred to as the "freedom songs." Again, there is a lot of overlapping between one era and the next. The type of gospel music most often sung in black churches then and now was birthed primarily in the depression era of the 1930s and 1940s. Because of that, this section will deal almost exclusively with the historic gospel music of that era.

Thomas A. Dorsey, referred to by many as "the father of gospel music," was one of the greatest influences on this historic type of gospel. Among the gospel songs to his credit are the well-known "Peace in the Valley," "Take My Hand, Precious Lord," and "The Lord Will Make a Way Somehow," all included in this section. Dorsey, the son of a minister, was an accomplished musician from an early age. As a young man he accompanied some of the most famous blues singers of all time, including Bessie Smith and Ma Rainey. In addition to the gospel music to his credit, Dorsey arranged and composed many blues songs. His adapting some of his blues style into his gospel compositions brought Dorsey a lot of criticism from the church. His songs were sometimes branded as "the devil's music." But Dorsey wasn't discouraged. "When I realized how hard some folks were fighting the gospel idea," he said, "I was determined to carry the banner." Because Dorsey refused to give up, he eventually wrote over eight hundred songs, and he lived to hear his once banished music ring out from the choir stands and congregations as well.

Although it is Dorsey who carries the honor of being called the father of gospel music, the influence of the Reverend Charles Albert Tindley in Dorsey's life cannot be overestimated. That influence is most obvious in a comparison of the two men's lyrics, where both deal with the inevitability of the storms and trials of life coupled with God's grace and faithfulness to bring them through. But the similarities between Dorsey and Tindley do not carry over into style. Tindley's songwriting was a hymn-based style of writing, while Dorsey broke away from that, establishing what is thought of as the gospel style. And yet to discuss the history and development of gospel music without mentioning Tindley is simply not possible. Tindley, whose birth date has been given as 1851, 1856, and 1859, was born to slave ancestors and was "hired out" as soon as he was old enough to work alongside the slaves on plantations. The plantation owners were not kind to him, forbidding him to go to church and discouraging his desire to learn to read. But Tindley persisted and taught himself to read the Bible, eventually becoming one of the most popular African-American Methodist preachers in history, ministering to black and white congregants alike.

Tindley's music wasn't just empty words. His songs came out of his own experiences, both from his life and from his study of the Bible. In fact, in many of his songs he "preached" a sermon, reaching some who might not listen to a biblical message delivered any other way. He told his stories through song in simple, direct words and melodies. He realized that gospel music was a singer's art, rather than a composer's. "Let Jesus Fix It for You," "Nothing Between," "Stand By Me," and "We'll Understand It Better By and By," all included in this section, are just a few of the songs penned by this powerful preacher/songwriter.

Gospel music was not the only type of music to evolve out of the hard times of the depression. The blues, a musical form which emerged from a type of music known as ragtime, also came into popularity during that time. In some ways, gospel music and the blues had much in common, in that both expressed the feelings and experiences of the era from which they were born. The primary difference between the two styles, however, was that the blues focused more on outward circumstances, making a sort of political statement on tragic social and economic conditions. Gospel music, although also a statement on the times, focused on the eternal hope of those caught in the social and economic difficulties of the era, and that hope was just as in the time of the writing of the spirituals—that God was the people's provider, their protector, their defender, their deliverer, their Savior. Because of this, the historic gospel songs centered on Jesus, whom people saw as the problem-solver, rather than on the problems themselves. Blues songs, despite the appeal of their deep sense of pathos, left both singers and listeners with a sense of hopelessness. Gospel music had the exact opposite effect, bringing its singers and listeners from hopelessness to hope. And in times of hardship, hope is a much sought-after commodity. The word "gospel," in fact, means "good news," and people in the midst of a bad situation are usually ripe for some good news.

It is not surprising, then, that gospel music has so deeply affected the music surrounding the entire black experience in America. It remains such a powerful and influential force today because the church is still the most powerful and influential institution within the African-American community. Bernice Johnson Reagon, editor of *We'll Understand It Better By and By: Pioneering African American Gospel Composers,* refers to gospel music as "by far the most vibrant, community-based musical genre within African America."

Gospel music is not just a collection of a type (or types) of songs. It is also a style of singing. Many of the gospel songs we are familiar with today originated in the words of hymns or spirituals, while other gospel songs are new compositions, performed in a variety of gospel styles. There are those who believe that the singing and performing of gospel music is something inborn, a talent or skill that simply cannot be taught effectively. In studying the lives of some of the greatest gospel artists, that belief often seems true, as most of them were literally born into or near the source of this music.

Gospel music historian Pearl Williams-Jones has said, "Inherent in this [gospel music] is the concept of African American folk rhetoric, folk expressions, bodily movement, charismatic energy, cadence, tonal range and timbre." With this explanation of gospel music in mind, it is easy to see why it is almost a misnomer to refer to those hearing others sing gospel as "listeners." Whether singing or hearing gospel music, almost all become involved at a deeper level than merely listening. Singers and hearers alike are participants in the exuberant experience of gospel, becoming caught up both in the exciting message of hope and in the passionate tone of the music.

Worship and praise are not spectator sports in gospel-singing churches. They are as real and natural as breathing to the congregants and singers alike—as real as the stories and histories behind the songs themselves.

Christ Is All

Words and Music by Kenneth Morris

1. I don't pos-sess hous- es or lands, fine clothes or jewel-ry,———

Sor-rows and cares in this old world my lot seems to be,———

But I have a Christ who paid the price way back on Cal-v'ry,———

Chorus

And Christ is all, all and all— this world to me.

Lead or High Soprano

Christ is all, He's ev - 'ry-thing to me, Christ is

Yes, Christ is all, He's ev - 'ry-thing to me,

all, He rules the land and sea, Christ is all with -

Yes, Christ is all, He rules the land and sea, Yes, Christ is all with -

out Him noth-ing could be, Christ is all, all and all _ this world to me.

out Him noth-ing could be, Christ is all, all and all _ this world to me.

2. *There are some folk who look and*
   long for this world's riches,
   There are some folk who look for
   pow'r, position too,
   But I have a Christ all in my life,
   this makes me happy, And . . .

3. *Yes, Christ is all, means more to*
   me than this world's riches,
   He is my sight, my guiding light
   through pathless seas,
   Yes, it's mighty nice to own a
   Christ who will my friend be,
   Yes . . .

*K*enneth Morris, the composer of "Christ Is All," was an African-American publisher, arranger, and composer, with more than 3,000 arranged songs to his credit. He entered the publishing business as an arranger in 1936. It was while he was in publishing that he composed his first gospel song, "I'll Be a Servant for the Lord," which was recorded by the Wings Over Jordan Choir. He also composed "Dig a Little Deeper in God's Love." "My God Is Real"—also called "Yes, God Is Real"—is another of his compositions, and is included in this section.

"Christ Is All" very typically reflects the political and social situation of the historic gospel era. In this song the author indicates that, materially, he possesses very little of any worth. And yet he also declares that he has everything that matters because he has Christ. His saying "I *have* . . . Christ" in itself denotes a very personal relationship with Christ in that the author dares to proclaim that he has Christ, rather than that he simply believes in Him. And that is the heart of this song. Kenneth Morris is making the statement that however difficult his lot in life may be, he recognizes it as temporary. He knows it will pass and he will never lose what really matters.

The depression era was a difficult time for almost everyone in America, with poverty crossing racial and economic boundaries. But African-Americans carried the brunt of the hardships. With jobs and housing scarce, they were the last in line to receive what little provision was available. If a job opportunity did happen to come along, preference was given to a white applicant, regardless of experience or capability. Seventy years had passed since the end of the Civil War and Emancipation, yet some of the descendants of slaves found themselves in as bad or worse economic situations than their ancestors.

It is little wonder then that African-Americans once again took comfort and encouragement from the Scriptures, which told of a God whose name was *Jehovah-jireh,* meaning "God provides." They looked to Him for everything, living out the words to this song, that "Christ is all, all and all this world to me."

Didn't It Rain

Words and Music by Roberta Martin

Verse (Soprano Solo - Choir hum)

1. It rained for-ty days and it rained for-ty nights, There
was-n't no land no-where in sights, God sent a ra-ven to
bring the news, He hoist his wings and a-way he flew. To the
East, to the West, To the North, to the
(Lis-ten to the rain) (Lis-ten to the rain) (Lis-ten to the rain)

South,　　　All— day,　　　All— night,

(Lis-ten to the rain)　　(Lis-ten to the rain)　　(Lis-ten to the rain)

Oh,　　　　　tell　me,　Did-n't　it

(Lis-ten　to　the　rain)　　(Lis-ten　to　it)　Did-n't　it

Choir

rain,————————　chil-dren,　　　　Rain,　oh,　my

(chil-dren didn't it)

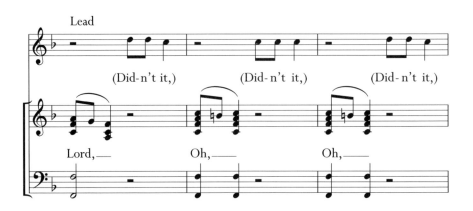

2. *It rained forty days, forty nights*
   without stopping,
   Noah was glad when the rain
   stopped dropping,
   When I get to heav'n going to put
   on my shoes,
   To walk 'round heav'n and tell
   the news.
   How it rained, in the East,
   How it rained in the West,
   All day, all night,
   Oh, (Listen to the rain)
   Tell me, (Listen to it)

3. *A knock at the window, a knock at*
   the door,
   They cried "Oh, Noah, please take
   on more,"
   But Noah cried out that "You're
   full of sin,
   My Lord's got the key, you can't
   get in!"
   Just listen! how it's raining,
   In the North, in the South,
   In the East, in the West
   Oh, (Listen to the rain)
   Tell me, (Listen to it)

*T*he lyrics to this song were penned by Roberta Martin (1907–1969), a singer, pianist, composer, arranger, and organizer of groups and choirs, who also went on to found and operate her own gospel music publishing house in Chicago. She is best known as an innovator of modern gospel music, successfully blending the African elements of energy, rhythms, spontaneous melody, and group participation with the Western European elements of harmony, form, and order. In other words, she effectively combined emotion with style. Many other gospel and secular singers have copied Martin's style of vocal control, phrasing, and timing ("leaning" on the beat).

"Didn't It Rain" actually began as a traditional spiritual. Like many of the spirituals that were adapted to gospel hymns, some of the lyrics were changed and the melodies altered somewhat through the years. I found three variations of the song, including one that is attributed to Lucy Matthews, who was born in 1928 and wrote four songs that were arranged by Roberta Martin. Written in the style of so many of the spirituals, "Didn't It Rain" depicts one of the best-known of Bible stories—that of Noah and the great flood. Because of the slaves' long-standing oral tradition of passing stories along in songs, they especially enjoyed singing the dramatic story of Noah and the ark, a story that has, in some form or other, been passed down through many cultures—Christian, Jewish, or otherwise—throughout the history the world. In addition, Africans and African-Americans have always had a great respect for the elements of nature, seeing in the rain, wind, lightning, and thunder the awesomeness of the Creator.

Not only has the African-American famously told biblical stories in the spirituals, but black preachers often sang their sermons. The telling of God's judgment on a people who refused to acknowledge Him through the singing of the story of the great flood was a powerful way not only to get a story across, but also to send a message of the need for repentance.

"Oh, Didn't It Rain," the original Negro spiritual arranged by H. T. Burleigh for solo voice and piano, tells the same story but with slightly different words.

> *Fo'ty days fo'ty nights when de rain kept a-fallin';*
> *De wicked clumb de tree,*
> *an' for help kept a-callin';*
> *For they heard de waters wailin'*
> *Didn't it rain, rain, didn't it rain*
> *Tell me Noah, didn't it rain*

Some climb'd de mountain,
Some climb'd de hill,
Some started sailin'
an' a-rowin' wid a will;
Some tried swimmin' an' I guess they're swimmin' still,
for they heard de waters roarin';
Didn't it rain, rain, didn't it rain
Tell me Noah, didn't it rain,
Didn't it rain.

It doesn't take much imagination for me to picture those slaves of old acting out this dramatic story as they sang of God's faithfulness to deliver those who loved Him, while the others were lost in the flood. As is true of all the gospel and spiritual songs, the story that is told always points to the hope of deliverance.

He Took My Sins Away

Words and Music by Mrs. M. J. Harris

1. I came to Je - sus, wea-ry, worn, and sad, He
took my sins a-way, He took my sins a-way, And

now His love has made my heart so glad, He took my sins a-

Chorus

way. He took my sins a-way, He took my sins a-way, And

keeps me sing-ing ev - 'ry day! I'm so glad He

took my sins a-way, He took my sins a - way.

2. The load of sin was more than I
     could bear,
   *He took my sins away, He took my
     sins away,*
   *And now on Him I roll my ev'ry
     care,*
   He took my sins away.

3. No condemnation have I in my
     heart,
   *He took my sins away, He took my
     sins away,*
   *His perfect peace He did to me
     impart,*
   He took my sins away.

4. *If you will come to Jesus Christ*   *And keep you happy in His love*
   today,   *each day,*
   He'll take your sins away, He'll   *He'll take your sins away.*
   take your sins away,

*H*e Took My Sins Away," written by Mrs. M. J. Harris, is a very popular song today, a favorite with the choirs I have led. Just a few years ago, Patrick Henderson, the gifted African-American musician who has arranged and written several well-known songs for contemporary music ministries, such as the West Los Angeles Church of God in Christ, arranged this gospel hymn into what is known as a "cooking" or "smoking" gospel song with a contemporary setting. It is known as a "jumping" song as well, because just the realization that one has been set free from the heavy load of sin creates a desire to leap, jump, and even fly!

The primary message of the church, during the depression era as well as today, was not simply that God was the provider when it came to financial and material needs, but also the provider when it came to forgiveness of sin, having sent His only Son for just that purpose. African-American Christians, despite their financial struggles, recognized that their greatest need was not employment or housing or even food and clothing, but relief from the heavy weight of sin. To know they were forgiven, to feel that weight lifted from their shoulders, was reason enough to sing—and sing they did, with great exuberance!

To say African-Americans were unprepared for the economic upheaval of the depression is an understatement at best. Already struggling with poverty, they were dropped even farther into the abyss by the financial plunge of 1929. It is difficult to understand how they survived that period at all, especially considering how far-reaching and devastating the financial effects were throughout all of America.

And yet survive they did. In fact, though black banks and businesses failed like all the others, the African-American community exhibited an amazing resilience. The church, long central in black American society, not only survived the depression, but grew in spite of it. Throughout the financial and social crises of the depression era and the lean years that followed, the church provided the internal stability needed for the people to press on, regardless of circumstances.

Hold to God's Unchanging Hand

Words by Jennie Wilson
Music by F. L. Eiland

1. Time is filled with swift tran - si - tion,

Naught of earth un - moved can stand,

Build your hopes on things e - ter - nal,

Hold to God's un - chang - ing hand!

Chorus

Hold   to   God's un-chang-ing hand!
(Hold   to   his hand)

Hold   to   God's un-chang-ing hand!
(Hold   to   his hand)

Build   your hopes on things e - ter - nal,

Hold   to God's un - chang - ing   hand!

2. *Trust in Him who will not leave*
   you,
   Whatsoever years may bring;
   If by earthly friends forsaken,
   Still more closely to Him cling!

3. *Covet not this world's vain riches,*
   That so rapidly decay;

Seek to gain the heav'nly treasures,
They will never pass away!

4. *When your journey is completed,*
   If to God you have been true,
   Fair and bright the home in glory,
   Your enraptured soul will view!

*J*ennie Wilson, who authored this song, was born in 1857 on a farm near South Whitley, Indiana, and spent most of the fifty-six years of her life in a wheelchair as a result of a spinal disease that struck her at age four. As an invalid, Jennie never attended school but studied at home, receiving some training in music. It is believed that in her lifetime she wrote more than 2,200 poems.

No one knew better than the African-American how unstable life could be. First there were their ancestors, uprooted from their homeland and transported thousands of miles across the sea to live a life of forced servitude. Then there were the emancipated slaves, who hoped for something better, only to see their hopes crushed by the reality of broken promises and lingering racism. Even though these freed slaves had been promised much—including forty acres and a mule for each one of them—those promises seldom if ever materialized. Most of these former slaves settled in the South, but many of them moved north, hoping for better opportunities. Those who remained in the South had to contend with the backlash of defeated and angry Confederates, while those in the North found out how difficult it was to compete against whites for jobs. Even the government agencies and services, such as the Freedmen's Bureau, which had been formed to help the emancipated slaves, soon dissolved. Finally, there were the black Americans of the depression era, who had fought for every financial and social gain, only to have them evaporate in the national tragedy of economic collapse.

In the midst of an ever-changing world, where little if anything could be depended upon to last through the next season of transition, how good it was to have something to hold on to that never changed! Where promises meant little or nothing and dreams were crushed long before they had a chance to become reality, what a comfort to know that there was indeed a hand that would never let go. The Bible says that Jesus Christ is the same—yesterday, today, and forever. Financial situations change. Social positions change. Family relationships change. Feelings and commitments change. Fortunes, dreams, and plans can all come crashing down. But one thing never changes. God's hand is always there—steady, strong, dependable. And that is what these struggling people held on to in the midst of yet another crisis in their history.

I Am on the Battlefield for My Lord

By Sylvana Bell and E. V. Banks
Arranged by Thomas A. Dorsey (1899–1993)

2. *I left my friends and kindred bound
    for the Promised Land,
   The grace of God upon me, the
    Bible in my hand,
   In distant lands I trod, Crying
    sinner come to God,
   I'm on the battlefield for my Lord.*

3. *Now when I met my Savior, I met
    Him with a smile,
   He healed my wounded spirit, And
    owned me as His child,
   Around the throne of grace, He
    appoints my soul a place,
   I'm on the battlefield for my Lord.*

*T*homas A. Dorsey, who arranged this song, was born into a musical family in 1899. His mother played the church organ, his uncle was a choir director, and his father was an itinerant Baptist preacher and revivalist, who often took his son along with him to different churches. Dorsey began writing gospel music in 1921 when he heard someone singing A. W. Nix's song "I Do, Don't You" at the National Baptist Convention in Chicago. His songwriting career was greatly influenced by the Reverend Charles Albert Tindley, as is evidenced in his frequent references to the "storms of life," a term often used by Tindley in his own songwriting. In this particular song, although Dorsey doesn't talk about storms, he does acknowledge the difficulties of life, referring to his service to God as "being on the battlefield for my Lord."

My grandfather, the Reverend Felix Rice Sims, was also familiar with being on the battlefield for his Lord. Grandfather Felix was born before the end of slavery and the freeing of the slaves in Alabama. Later, he attended Talladega College, a land-grant school in Alabama run by the Congregational Church after the Civil War. It was there that he met my grandmother, Emma Evaline Griffin Sims.

Reverend Felix Sims became a Congregational minister. He and my grandmother also became postmaster and postmistress of the post office in Talladega. Feeling the need for more liberty and freedom in his ministry and pastorate, he left the Congregational Church to join with the African Methodist Episcopal Church.

Felix and Emma had five children—two daughters, Pauline Jewett and Miriam Blanche; and three sons: David, who became a bishop in the A.M.E. Church; and George T. and Yancey Lee, my father, who both became pastors and presiding elders in the church.

Grandfather Felix, who died long before I was born, served as pastor of "Big Bethel" A.M.E. Church in Atlanta, Georgia, and Bethel Church in Savannah, Georgia, among others, in the first decade of this century. His later years were spent serving as presiding elder in Georgia, and as a circuit rider. When he went throughout the countryside he packed a pistol. Although he believed he was "clothed in the armor of God" as a good soldier of the cross, he also knew that the country roads and woods were dangerous for him. An African-American, particularly one wearing a suit and traveling in such places, was a constant target of threats from mobs and gangs, which were the forerunners of the Ku Klux Klan.

Throughout his time on earth, Grandfather Felix served his Lord relentlessly and zealously. He, like Dorsey and so many others, truly knew what it meant to be on the battlefield for the Lord.

I Bowed on My Knees and Cried Holy

Words by Nettie Dudley Washington
Music by E. M. Dudley Cantwell

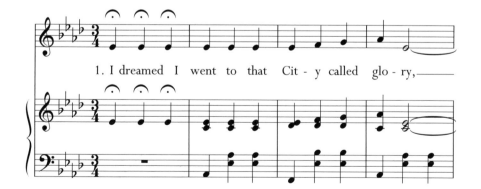

1. I dreamed I went to that Cit - y called glo - ry,—

So bright and so fair;_____ When I
en-tered the gate I cried Ho - ly,_____ The
an - gels all met me there,_____ They
car-ried me from Man-sion to Man-sion,_____ And

Ho - ly,_____ Ho - ly,_____ I

clapped my hands and sang glo - ry,_____

ritard.

Glo - ry to the Son of God._____

2. *I thought when I entered that
   City,
   My loved ones all knew me well;
   They showed me all through
   Heaven,
   The scenes are too numerous to tell.*

   *They showed me Abraham, Isaac,
   and Jacob,
   Mark, Luke, and Timothy,
   But I said I want to bow down and
   give praise
   To the One who died for me.*

3. *I thought when I saw my Savior,*
   Oh! glory to God!
   I just fell right down before Him,
   Singing praise the name of the Lord.
   I bowed down and worshipp'd
      Jehovah
   My friend of Calvary,
   For I wanted to give praise to
      Jesus,
   For saving a sinner like me.

4. *I thought when I saw my dear*
      Savior,
   There seated on His throne,
   Oh, the wonder that He could
      love me,
   and call me His very own.
   I bowed down and worshipped this
      Savior,
   My friend of Calvary;
   And I wanted to praise Him forever
   For saving one like me.

*A*s lovely and sacred as it is, and as popular as gospel music was and still is today, it hasn't always been wholeheartedly accepted in all arenas. The strong social message of many gospel songs was rejected, even snubbed, in certain areas of Christianity, particularly where there was concern about keeping the gospel message a purely spiritual one. Some of the more conservative elements of the church saw it as a dangerous influence, creeping in to water down the true gospel of Christ and replace it with nothing more than social commentaries. "I Bowed on My Knees and Cried Holy," one of the most beloved songs of the era, stands in stark contrast to that criticism. Most sacred and reverent, this beautiful song was written by Nettie Dudley Washington and E. M. Dudley Cantwell.

The words to this gospel song paint a majestic picture of Heaven, as the singer is carried by angels throughout the streets of gold, being shown glorious mansions and meeting the saints of old—Abraham, Isaac, Jacob, Mark, Luke, Timothy. And yet the song's author declares that, as wonderful as all these sights may be, the most desired sight of all is to see Jesus. The author's greatest desire is to meet the Master and to bow at His feet in reverent adoration and thanksgiving. The trials and tribulations of life on earth aren't even mentioned. The focus is entirely on Jesus, whose death paid the price of admission to the celestial city.

It would be impossible to find fault with the words to this song. Certainly the text is more than a "social" or watered-down gospel. Today, "I Bowed on My Knees and Cried Holy" is a favorite and oft-sung selection in churches of all races and denominations.

I Love the Lord

Traditional Spiritual

1. I love the Lord, He heard my cries, And pit-ied ev-'ry groan; Long as I live, When trou-bles rise, I'll has-ten to His throne.

2. I love the Lord, He bowed His ear,
   And chased my grief away;
   O let my heart no more despair
   While I have breath to pray.

3. The Lord beheld me sore distressed;
   He bade my pains remove;
   Return, my soul, to God, thy rest,
   For thou hast known His love.

*T*his traditional song is taken from Psalm 116:1–2, which says, "I love the Lord, because He has heard my voice and my supplications. Because He has inclined His ear to me, Therefore I will call upon Him as long as I live." It was, in fact, arranged in a contemporary style by Richard Small-wood and recorded by Whitney Houston for the movie soundtrack of *The Preacher's Wife*. Smallwood's name is one of the most recognizable in contemporary gospel today. He has been honored by the Smithsonian Institution, has received the Washington, D.C., Mayoral Art Award, and his performances include appearances at the White House and the Kennedy Center. Smallwood was honored in 1993 when Washington, D.C., mayor Sharon Pratt Kelly proclaimed April 18 and 19 of that year to be "Richard Smallwood Days."

"I Love the Lord" finds its roots in the "line hymn" or "meter hymn" of the late nineteenth century. The establishment of what is often referred to as "black meter music" took place over a period of time spanning slavery and freedom. It was a type of singing that bridged the slavery period with the Reconstruction period and on into the early part of the twentieth century.

The excitement and passion of this period of time lent itself naturally to a livelier form of music. Because of their freshness and vitality, the old English Watts- and Wesley-style hymns from two centuries earlier provided the basis for this new form of music. It was not that the meter hymn replaced the spiritual in the African-American church; it simply embodied the social and religious changes taking place during that time. As in the days of slavery, the emancipated slaves adapted their music to fit their situations, singing about their daily lives and circumstances. The repertoire of African-American Christians was growing and changing even as the conditions of their lives changed.

I'd Rather Have Jesus

Words by Rhea F. Miller
Music by George Beverly Shea

I'd rath-er have Je-sus than sil-ver or gold, I'd rath-er be His than have rich-es un-told;— I'd rath-er have Je-sus than hous-es or lands, I'd rath-er be led by His nail-pierced hand.

Chorus

Than to be the king of a vast do - main Or be held in sin's dread sway;⸺ I'd rath - er have Je - sus than an - y - thing This⸺ world af - fords to - day.⸺

2. I'd rather have Jesus than men's
    applause,
   I'd rather be faithful to His dear
    cause;
   I'd rather have Jesus than
    worldwide fame,
   I'd rather be true to His holy
    name.

3. He's fairer than lilies of rarest
    bloom,
   He's sweeter than honey from out
    the comb;
   He's all that my hungering spirit
    needs,
   I'd rather have Jesus and let Him
    lead.

*G*eorge Beverly Shea, who wrote the music for this song, is one of America's most beloved gospel singers. Just the mention of his name brings to mind the decades of Billy Graham Crusades of which his featured solos have been such an integral part. His rich bass voice and his uncompromising Christian testimony have been a blessing to countless thousands of viewers and listeners over the years.

Raised in a devout Christian home, Shea gave his life over to the service of Christ at a very early age. His faithfulness and commitment have been rewarded as his opportunities to minister in song have taken him all over the world.

"I wrote 'I'd Rather Have Jesus' in 1933," Shea said. "As I sat one evening playing the piano, my mother brought to me a piece of paper on which was written a poem by Rhea Miller. She thought it to be a very wonderful poem and wanted me to read it. She then asked me to try my hand at writing a melody for it. I began to play as a melody came to me. I then sang and played for the first time 'I'd Rather Have Jesus.'"

Because of his rich voice and incredible talent, Shea has had many lucrative offers through the years, particularly in the beginning of his career. However, he turned them down for the privilege of being a "singing servant" for God, whom he preferred over all others. We see that preference throughout the lyrics to this song. The songwriter proclaims a preference for Jesus over "silver or gold . . . houses or lands . . . men's applause . . . worldwide fame." How well I can relate to that! I too had many opportunities in my younger years to perform on stages worldwide. Some of those opportunities I seized, pursuing them for a time with great success. However, I found that success—and even the possibility of material wealth—empty, the applause of men meaningless. It was only in returning to God who gifted me to sing that I found any true fulfillment and peace. I can honestly say, along with Rhea F. Miller and George Beverly Shea, "I'd rather have Jesus!"

I'll Be Caught Up to Meet Him in the Air

Words and Music by Clarence E. Hatcher

One day, one day, I'm go-ing where Je - sus

is. One day, one day, I'm go-ing where Je - sus

is. One day, one - day, I'm go-ing where Je - sus

is. I'll be caught up to meet Him in the air.

%𝄋 **Chorus**

I'll be caught up to meet Him. I'll be caught up to greet Him.

Joy and hap - pi - ness will be mine When we

meet 'round the throne in glo - ry Tell - ing the bless - ed sto - ry.

I'm press - ing on - ward to that glo - rious day.

1. Je - sus,   Je - sus,   Je - sus saved me one   day.   Je -

sus, Je - sus,   Je - sus saved me one day. Je - sus,   Je - sus,

D.S.

Je - sus saved me one day. I'll be caught up   to meet Him in the air.

(Use at end of last chorus)   rit.

I'll be caught up   to meet my Je - sus   in___ the   air.___

2. One day, one day,
   I'll leave this house of clay.
   One day, one day,
   I'll leave this house of clay.
   One day, one day,
   I'll leave this house of clay.
   I'll be caught up to meet Him in
      the air.

3. I want to see
   King Jesus first of all.
   I want to see
   King Jesus first of all.

   I want to see
   King Jesus first of all.
   I'll be caught up to meet Him in
      the air.

4. Oh bye, and bye
   I'm going for a chariot ride.
   Oh bye, and bye
   I'm going for a chariot ride.
   Oh bye, and bye
   I'm going for a chariot ride.
   I'll be caught up to meet Him in
      the air.

*A*lthough life was hard for African-Americans when this song was writ-ten by Clarence E. Hatcher, we see within the song a promise that some-day "joy and happiness will be mine." As is typical of so many of the gospel and spiritual songs, the authors were looking forward, pressing in, greatly anticipating something better. The title of this great gospel song refers to what is known as the rapture of the church, when Christ returns "in the twinkling of an eye" to take or "snatch" His church out of the world. It is taken from the words of 1 Thessalonians 4:16–18:

> For the Lord himself will come down from Heaven with a com-manding shout, with the call of the archangel, and with the trumpet call of God. First, all the Christians who have died will rise from their graves. Then, together with them, we who are still alive and remain on the earth will be caught up in the clouds to meet the Lord in the air and remain with him forever. So comfort and encourage each other with these words.

For nearly two thousand years the church has looked forward to that great day of Christ's return, particularly during times of great trials and tribulations. The periods of the spirituals and gospel songs were no excep-tions. If ever people needed to "comfort and encourage each other with these words," it was during those times.

Although the experiences of slavery in America were limited to African-Americans, the financial and social struggles of the depression were not. The effects of that difficult time in our country's history were felt by nearly everyone. But without a doubt, black citizens were more adversely affected than most others. With many of them already poor when the stock market crashed in 1929, their situations quickly went from bad to worse. It seemed that, once again, circumstances were as bleak as anyone could ever imagine. It is not surprising then that the anticipation of being "caught up to meet Him in the air" at any moment was indeed a blessed hope to hang onto.

I'll Fly Away

Words and Music by Albert E. Brumley

1. Some glad morn-ing when this life is o'er, ——
I'll (fly a-way) fly a-way. (fly a-way)
To a home on God's ce-les-tial shore, ——

2. *When the shadows of this life have
   grown,
   I'll fly away.
   Like a bird from prison bars has
   flown,
   I'll fly away.*

3. *Just a few more weary days and
   then,
   I'll fly away.
   To a land where joys shall never
   end,
   I'll fly away.*

*A*lbert E. Brumley, who authored "I'll Fly Away," one of his first compositions, is considered one of the nation's leading gospel songwriters, having written more than six hundred songs in all. Not only has this song been sung in churches and auditoriums of all sizes, it has even been performed by one of the most popular symphony orchestras in the country. Brumley is the only gospel songwriter with four albums of his music recorded on major labels.

As in "I'll Be Caught Up to Meet Him in the Air," "I'll Fly Away," looks forward to leaving this life on earth behind and going on to a much better life with Jesus in Heaven. The primary difference between the two songs is that "I'll Be Caught Up to Meet Him in the Air" deals with Christ's return to catch away the entire church, while "I'll Fly Away" focuses more on the individual believer's death. Both songs, however, indicate a strong belief that moving on from this earth is something to be anticipated with longing, rather than with dread. In "I'll Fly Away," we see the author's excitement at the prospect in the very first line: "Some glad morning when this life is o'er."

It is easy to see how songs that focused on the next life—a much better life—would flourish in a time of extreme difficulty and poverty. Gospel lyrics themselves are an expression of the things that matter most to people who seem to have the least. People without financial hardships are preoccupied with issues beyond the daily needs of food and shelter, so they are less likely to write songs about such basic things. But for those who face an ongoing struggle simply to survive, promises for a better life to come are very appealing. Focusing on those promises helps relieve the temptation to focus solely on the problems. For that very reason, these songs were more than intellectual expressions of social or cultural situations. The creation of this music involved emotional investment from preachers, songwriters, and worshippers alike.

Another probable reason for this song's popularity is that the enslaved were fascinated with the concept of flying. As in "All God's Chillun Got Shoes," which speaks of flying all over God's Heaven, flying represented freedom to these indentured people. "Swing Low, Sweet Chariot" also portrays a chariot coming down to pick up God's people and carry them through the air to Heaven. But flying was more than just something these early African-Americans looked forward to in the next life. It was a feeling they experienced when they began to sing. As they "felt the Spirit" during their praise and worship times, they also felt themselves being carried away and above their circumstances, "flying" above the earthly struggles that held them down. This gave them a sense of freedom and victory, not only over their circumstances but over their oppressors as well.

I've Got a Feeling

Traditional Spiritual

1. I've_____ got a feel - ing_____ ev - 'ry -

thing's gon - na be al - right,_____ O,_____

2. *Jesus already told me, ev'rything's
gonna be alright, . . .*

3. *The Holy Ghost has confirmed it,
ev'rything's gonna be alright, . . .*

*L*ike many of the spirituals, "I've Got a Feeling" is listed as a traditional song, meaning a song that came forth spontaneously, possibly in a prayer and praise meeting, and has no specific known author. It has become a community-owned song, as singers and listeners alike relate to its words of assurance and adopt its message.

How many times I have found myself in the midst of tragedies, emergencies, crises, seemingly running around in circles, trying to find an answer, only to sense God calling me aside. "Be still, and know that I am God," He would whisper from the Scriptures. "Hush. Calm down. I'm still in control. Everything is going to be all right."

Like a child having received assurance from a loving parent, I would relax. The crisis or emergency would still be there, needing to be handled, but the tension was gone. I knew that, regardless of how desperate the situation, everything truly was going to be all right.

That was undoubtedly the message the authors of "I've Got a Feeling" were attempting to convey through this jumping, dancing gospel song. This particular song is sung often, in many churches, in many denominations, by all races, on many stages, and in many homes across this land. It is impossible to sing this song for any length of time and with any depth of enthusiasm and remain despondent or depressed. True, there has always been some criticism within the church of placing too much confidence in "feelings," and rightfully so. But when those feelings are based on God's promises, Christians can enjoy them to the fullest—and sing about them with abandon.

The pre–Civil War slaves and the depression-era African-Americans were all too familiar with the very real feelings of prejudice, injustice, degradation, humiliation, and deprivation. To be able to "sing themselves happy" with the great truth that, ultimately, everything would be all right was a powerful healing remedy for their weary souls and bodies.

Jesus, the Light of the World

Arranged by George D. Elderkin

1. Hark! the her - ald an - gels sing,

Je - sus, the Light of the world;

Glo - ry to the new - born King,

Je - sus, the Light of the world.

Chorus

We'll walk in the light, beau - ti - ful light,

Come where the dew - drops of mer - cy are bright,

Shine all a - round us by day and by night,

Je - sus, the Light of the world. A - men

2. *Joyful, all ye nations, rise,*
 Jesus, the Light of the world;
 Join the triumph of the skies,
 Jesus, the Light of the world.

3. *Christ, by highest heav'n adored,*
 Jesus, the Light of the world;
 Christ, the everlasting Lord,
 Jesus, the Light of the world.

4. *Hail the heav'n born Prince of*   *Hail the Sun of Righteousness!*
   Peace!   *Jesus, the Light of the world.*
   Jesus, the Light of the world;

*A*rranged by George D. Elderkin, "Jesus, the Light of the World" is a wonderful marching song. Gospel choirs in the African-American church just love to march down the aisle singing this triumphant song, which was adapted from Charles Wesley's text of the hymn "Hark, the Herald Angels Sing." Wesley's hymn is a Christmas favorite, and is sung every year around the world. Wesley wrote this hymn early in his life, sometime before 1739, and within a year of his conversion to Christianity. The inspired words reflect Wesley's excitement over his new relationship with God. Wesley's original poem had ten stanzas, but not all the verses appear in the hymn we sing today. This is because most editors have taken out the last four stanzas, which were primarily theological. Some of the remaining lines have also been changed in an effort to improve the original poetry.

That edited version of Wesley's hymn is what we see reflected in the words to "Jesus, the Light of the World." The song has been adapted to the people and circumstances of the times. It is also reminiscent of some of the earlier spirituals, such as "Walk You in the Light" and "Let de Heb'n-light Shine on Me":

> *Let de Heb'n-light shine on me,*
> *Let de Heb'n-light shine on me,*
> *For low is de way to de upper bright worl',*
> *Let de Heb'n-light shine on me.*
>
> *Oh, brother, you mus' bow so low,*
> *Oh, brother, you mus' bow so low,*
> *For low is de way to de upper bright worl',*
> *Let de Heb'n-light shine on me.*

As varied as these songs may be in wording, the message is still the same: Jesus is the light of the world, as proclaimed in John 8:12: "I am the light of the world. If you follow me, you won't be stumbling through the darkness, because you will have the light that leads to life." This message is

often proclaimed in the African-American church through the singing of
this gospel song. And this song has been sung for years at many of the
church's traditional Christmas candlelight services.

Just a Closer Walk with Thee

Traditional Spiritual
Arranged by Kenneth Morris

Just   a clos-er walk with Thee;   Grant it, Je-sus, if you   please,

Dai - ly walk-ing close with Thee,   Let it   be, dear Lord, let it   be.

1. I   am weak but Thou art   strong,   Je - sus, keep me from all wrong,

I'll   be sat-is-fied as   long,   as I walk, Let me walk close with Thee.

2. *Through this world of toils and
   snares,
   If I falter, Lord, who cares,
   Who with me my burden shares,
   None but Thee, dear Lord, none
   but Thee.*

3. *When my feeble life is o'er,
   Time for me won't be no more,
   Guide me gently, safely o'er,
   To Thy kingdom shore, to Thy
   shore.*

*T*his song was arranged by Kenneth Morris in 1940, and by the end of the year it had swept the country, becoming one of the most popular gospel songs of its time. It has now been translated into eleven languages. In Morris's own words, the performance of "Just a Closer Walk with Thee" at the National Baptist Convention in 1944 "put us on the map."

A lot of controversy exists over the authorship of this song, with accusations that it does not belong to Morris. Morris, however, claims he arranged it from an old spiritual. "It was a plantation song," he explains, "and I heard it and liked it so well that I came and made an arrangement of it." Morris originally heard it sung by a choir at a conference in Kansas City. When he asked the choir director where it came from, the director did not know, explaining only that he had heard it all his life. Morris then went and arranged the song, and the first version of it put in print was his. After presenting it to the National Baptist Convention in 1944, "everybody was using it," Morris said. "[However], at that particular time, we weren't too careful about getting copyrights so it was stolen from me."

My first recording was of a single of this beautiful gospel song. I sang it solo at the New Jersey Annual Conference of the AME Church in Camden, in 1947, when I was about six or seven years old. Even at that young age, I could sense myself drawing closer to God as I sang these words. It was very encouraging to me to know that, though I was small and weak, He was strong, and it was His strength that would keep me from wrong. As young as I was, I believe that as I sang this song I was singing a prayer to God—a prayer which He has faithfully answered through the years in continually drawing me into a closer walk with Him.

Let Jesus Fix It for You

Words and Music by Charles Albert Tindley (c. 1851–1933)

1. If your life in days gone by, Has not been good and true,—
In your own way no long-er try, But let Him fix it for you.—

Chorus

Let Je-sus fix it for you,— He knows just what to do;— When-ev-er you pray, let Him have His way, And He will fix it for you.

2. Perhaps your temper is to blame,
For many wrongs you do,
Take it to God in Jesus' name,
And He will fix it for you.

3. If in your home the trouble is,
The course you should pursue,
Go talk with God, your hand
in His,
And He will fix it for you.

4. *And if some sin your soul hath*
   bound
   With cords you can't undo,
   At Jesus' feet go lay it down,
   And He will fix it for you.

5. *Maybe to you the world is dark,*
   And comforts far and few,
   Let Jesus own and rule your heart,
   And He will fix it for you.

*C*harles Albert Tindley was born around 1851 in Berlin in the Eastern Shore area of Maryland. Tindley, a songwriter, preacher, and publisher of both sermons and songs, is considered to have been a major force in the development of gospel music. Reverend Tindley had a strong influence on many of the early gospel composers, including Lucie E. Campbell, Thomas A. Dorsey, Reverend William Herbert Brewster, and Roberta Martin. Many of his songs have become classics of the African-American sacred music tradition.

As well as being one of Tindley's most beloved compositions, "Let Jesus Fix It for You" is also one of gospel singer Shirley Caesar's best-known songs. Born in 1938 in Durham, North Carolina, Shirley sang in church choirs as a child and was singing professionally by the time she was fourteen. She became a full-time evangelist in 1958, joining a group called the Caravans. She later formed her own group in 1966 called the Shirley Caesar Singers, and soon became known as the leading female gospel singer of her generation. Although her style of singing was often described as "rock-gospel," she limited her selections to sacred music.

"Let Jesus Fix It for You" is a song that speaks to the despondency and despair of a situation that seems to have no solution. Reverend Tindley once said, "You know, the only way you can really become defeated on your way to Heaven is to allow life's difficulties to get inside of you, and to turn you sour." This song is a testimony to his belief that "One of the things that we have to do—we must do—is to make sure that we do not try to take vengeance. That if we belong to Him, then He in His own time will take care of the situation."

There is a peace and a patience in this type of thinking that comes only from "going through the fire." Most of us, if we have to endure a trial or a problem for even the shortest amount of time, find ourselves stewing and fretting and becoming frustrated and discouraged as we try to fix the problem ourselves. There is no peace and patience in trying to fix something that, for us, is unfixable. But to turn those situations over to God brings great peace indeed. Tindley, like so many other African-Americans who endured slavery or the depression or discrimination and racism, was a master at walking in that peace.

Former ambassador to the United Nations Dr. Alan L. Keyes, in his book *Masters of the Dream: The Strength and Betrayal of Black America,* describes the early freedom fighters as those who "never surrendered the kernel of their humanity or their hope for a better day." The freedom fighters included those who endured the social pressures and financial hardships of the depression era, who composed, sang, and lived such gospel songs as "Let Jesus Fix It for You," believing Him to do just that.

The Lord Will Make a Way Somehow

Words and Music by Thomas A. Dorsey (1899–1993)

1. Like a ship that's toss'd and driv-en,—

Bat-tered by an an-gry sea,—

When the storms of life are rag - ing____ And their

fu - ry falls on me, I won-der what I have

done____ That makes this race so hard to run, Then I

say to my soul, take cour-age,____ The

Lord will make a way some - how.____

Chorus

The Lord will make a way some - how,

When be - neath the cross I bow; He will take a - way each

sor - row, Let Him have your bur - dens now;

When the load bears down so heav - y, — The

weight is shown up-on my brow, There's a sweet re-lief in

know-ing,— O, The Lord will make a way some-how.

2. *Try to do my best in service,*
   Try to live the best I can,
   When I choose to do the right thing,
   Evil's present on ev'ry hand,
   I look up and wonder why
   That good fortune pass me by,
   Then I say to my soul, be patient,
   The Lord will make a way
        somehow.

3. *Often there's misunderstanding*
   Out of all the good I do,
   Go to friends for consolation
   And I find them complaining too.
   So many nights I toss in pain,
   Wondering what the day will bring,
   But I say to my heart, don't worry,
   The Lord will make a way
        somehow.

*T*he Lord Will Make a Way Somehow" is another of Thomas Dorsey's famous compositions—and there are many! Dorsey's standing as "the father of gospel music" is due at least in part to the tremendous number of gospel songs attributed to his name. Over the span of his career, Dorsey wrote and arranged about eight hundred songs, including blues and popular music prior to his gospel writing. But his road wasn't always an easy one.

Dorsey was a controversial figure in his day, having coined the term "gospel music" in 1921. Preachers were disturbed by the term, saying, "You can't sing no gospel . . . you can only preach it." Some even called it "sin music," relating it to jazz, blues, and show business. Gospel music was different from the hymns and spirituals they knew and loved. As a result, there was opposition to its acceptance. Some ministers preached against it; others went even further. Several gospel singers—including Dorsey and Mahalia Jackson—were put out of or barred from churches. Most preachers in Dorsey's day failed to understand or realize the spiritual quality and impact of his music, and therefore rejected or ostracized it. But Dorsey persevered, believing that the Lord would "make a way somehow." Borrowing five dollars to send out five hundred copies of his song "If You See My Savior" to churches all across the land, he waited three long years before he got his first order. It is obvious that being a pioneer in anything—including the father of gospel music—isn't always an easy assignment. And yet, gospel music, as well as gospel singers, persevered, weathering the storms and refusing to give up. Today, gospel music is firmly established not only among black churches, but throughout the Christian community of all races and nationalities.

My God Is Real (Yes, God Is Real)

Words and Music by Kenneth Morris

thing, That God is real for I can feel Him deep with-in.

Chorus

Yes, God is real, real in my soul;———— Yes, God is

real, for He has washed and made me whole; His love for

me is like pure gold, Yes, God is real, for I can feel Him in my soul.

2. *Some folk may doubt, some folk*
   may scorn,
   All can desert and leave me alone,
   But as for me I'll take God's part,
   For God is real and I can feel Him
   in my heart.

3. *I cannot tell just how you felt*
   When Jesus took your sins away,
   But since that day, yes, since that
   hour,
   God has been real, for I can feel
   His holy pow'r.

*S*oon after Kenneth Morris's performance of his arrangement of "Just a Closer Walk with Thee" was so well received at the National Baptist Convention in 1944, he had four other major hits at the annual conventions that followed: "Jesus I Love You," "Christ Is All," "Don't You Care," and "My God Is Real (Yes, God Is Real)." Written by Morris in 1944, "My God Is Real" was his most popular composition.

Morris, who was one of gospel music's most successful composers, took his music very seriously. He believed that music was the one form of expression common to all people, and that the commonality of music could cross racial and social lines and bring people together in a harmony they might not find any other way. He referred to music as the "universal language," believing that even those from different countries and backgrounds and dialects could "readily grasp [another's] sentiments and moods through his music."

Morris's belief that "music speaks to the soul of man" is a belief shared by most African-Americans through the centuries, and explains to a large degree why music has always been such an important part of our culture. Because of that belief, as well as Morris's strong Christian faith, he was adamant that we be careful what we say through music.

Kenneth Morris never wrote about anything he considered frivolous or unimportant. The themes of his compositions were very real to him, and none expressed the reality of his faith more surely than this song. He was conveying the message deep down in his soul, a certainty of his belief that was shared by so many others who readily related to his declaration that "God is real." He based all of his compositions on that foundation, and on that foundation his songs were warmly received and acclaimed.

My Soul Loves Jesus

Words and Music by Bishop Charles H. Mason (1866–1961)

1. My soul loves Je-sus,— my soul loves Je-sus,— my— soul loves Je-sus; bless His name.— My soul loves Je-sus,— my soul loves Je-sus, my— soul loves Je-sus;— bless— His name.

2. He's a wonder in my soul, He's a
   wonder in my soul,
   He's a wonder in my soul; bless
   His name.
   He's a wonder in my soul, He's a
   wonder in my soul,
   He's a wonder in my soul; bless
   His name.

3. My soul seeks to please Him, my
   soul seeks to please Him,
   My soul seeks to please Him; bless
   His name.
   My soul seeks to please Him, my
   soul seeks to please Him,
   My soul seeks to please Him; bless
   His name.

A simple yet most beautiful song of the twentieth century in the tradition of the earlier spirituals, the words and music of "My Soul Loves Jesus" were penned by Bishop Charles H. Mason. Mason lived from 1866 to 1961 and was the founder of the Church of God in Christ (COGIC), a black Pentecostal denomination. It was from COGIC and other Pentecostal (sometimes known as Holiness or Sanctified) churches that came into existence at about the turn of the century, and especially the work of Mason, that much of gospel music got its style. The African-American Baptists were already singing their lining hymns, as well as many of the spirituals from the slave era. But as popular as that music was, it lacked the intensity that was predominant in the Pentecostal churches that were birthed during that period of revival, particularly the famous Azusa Street Revival. Black believers were immediately attracted to the joy of the spirited choruses and refrains coming out of the Pentecostal churches. They found the music exciting and perfectly suited to their tastes. Before long they had accepted it as their own.

Whether "My Soul Loves Jesus" was a song Bishop Mason actually sat down and composed or whether it simply burst forth as a spontaneous spiritual song, I don't know. Either is certainly possible. It was not at all unusual at that time—or even today, for that matter—for someone in the midst of a church service or prayer meeting to break out into song. Having been moved by the Holy Spirit and feeling overwhelmed with love for God, the singer would simply express inmost, heartfelt feelings of love, adoration, and praise. Singing a spontaneous new "love song" to the Lord Jesus is perfectly exemplified by the title song of this book, "Ev'ry Time I Feel de Spirit."

Nothing Between

Words and Music by Charles Albert Tindley (c. 1851–1933)

1. Noth - ing be - tween my soul and the Sav - ior,

Naught of this world's de - lu - sive dream;

I have re - nounced all sin - ful pleas - ure,

Je - sus is mine! There's noth - ing be - tween.

Chorus

Noth - ing be - tween my soul and the Sav - ior,

So that His bless - ed face may be seen;

Noth - ing pre - vent - ing the least of His fa - vor;

Keep the way clear! Let noth - ing be - tween.

2. Nothing between, like worldly
pleasure!
Habits of life, though harmless
they seem,
Must not my heart from Him ever
sever,
He is my all! There's nothing
between.

3. Nothing between, like pride or
station,
Self or friends shall not
intervene;

Though it may cost me much
tribulation,
I am resolved! There's nothing
between.

4. Nothing between, e'en many hard
trials,
Though the whole world against
me convene;
Watching with prayer and much
self-denial,
Triumph at last, with nothing
between!

*F*rom humble beginnings, Charles Albert Tindley, the author of "Nothing Between" and many other beloved gospel songs, went on to become one of the most popular preachers of his time. In fact, Tindley, who had once worked as janitor of the Calvary Methodist Episcopal Church in Philadelphia, was called in 1902 to pastor that very church. This church then prospered so greatly under his leadership that something had to be done to accommodate the large crowds, black and white, who came to hear him preach. Several larger sanctuaries eventually were built, and in spite of Tindley's many protests, in 1924 the new church building was renamed the Tindley Temple Methodist Church.

Occasionally Tindley was known to tell the stories behind the writing of his songs. The story behind "Nothing Between" is quite unusual, showing that inspiration can come in the most unexpected ways. It seems Tindley was doing some writing out in his backyard one day in 1905 when suddenly a gust of wind came up. The wind blew a small piece of trash onto his lap, and it landed between his pen and the paper he was writing on, blocking his view of the words. As he stopped writing to remove the piece of trash, he thought, "Now, that's what sin does, comes between a person and God." He then gave up working on his previous piece and proceeded to write this song.

The Bible tells us that "if our conscience is clear, we can come to God with bold confidence." The message of this song is that we must allow nothing to come between ourselves and God—we must keep our conscience clear. It is a directive that Tindley not only wrote about, but sought to live out in his own life as well.

Peace in the Valley

Words and Music by Thomas A. Dorsey (1899–1993)

1. I am tir - ed and wea - ry but I must toil on Till the Lord comes to call me a - way,

Where the morn - ing is bright and the Lamb is the light, And the night is as fair as the day.

Chorus

There'll be peace in the val - ley for me some - day, There'll be

peace   in the val - ley for   me.   I   pray no more sor - row and

sad - ness or   trou - ble will   be, There'll be   peace—   in the

val - ley   for   me.————— 2. There'll be me.————

2. There the flow'rs will be blooming,
   the grass will be green,
   And the skies will be clear and
   serene,
   The sun ever shines, giving one
   endless beam,
   And no clouds there will ever be
   seen.

3. There the bear will be gentle, the
   wolf will be tame,
   And the lion will lay down by the
   lamb,

   The host from the wild will be led
   by a Child,
   I'll be changed from the creature
   I am.

4. No headaches or heartaches or
   misunderstands,
   No confusion or trouble won't be,
   No frowns to defile, just a big
   endless smile,
   There'll be peace and contentment
   for me.

*T*homas A. Dorsey wrote hundreds of songs in his lifetime, two of his masterpieces being "Precious Lord" and "Peace in the Valley." Both of these songs were written in 1932 after the tragic death of his wife and newborn son. Some of the most beautiful music of all time has been born out of intense grief and suffering; spirituals and gospel songs are no exception.

The great singer Mahalia Jackson included many of Dorsey's songs in her repertoire, singing them with such depth of feeling that listeners were sure she had actually experienced the author's pain. Jackson brought these songs to life with her passionate performances. The music industry recognized the power of this type of music, and often showcased gospel singers in nightclubs and theaters. But despite lucrative offers for nightclub appearances, Mahalia Jackson refused to perform in that setting, insisting that it was not the proper place "for my kind of singing."

The influence of Charles Albert Tindley on Thomas Dorsey is evident in Dorsey's lyric style, particularly in his references to the storms of life and of the good that is produced through the overcoming of adversity. In turn, Dorsey's influence on gospel music in its entirety is unequaled, to the extent that much of the gospel music from this era was referred to by Dorsey's name. In *Somebody's Calling My Name,* Wyatt T. Walker says about Dorsey, "So large did the influence of Dorsey loom over the world of Gospel that during the forties and fifties most Gospel music was referred to as 'Dorsey's.'" Writer Horace C. Boyer echoes that statement:

"Not only did he [Dorsey] begin the contemporary tradition, but he is so imposing that there were periods during the Forties and Fifties when all gospel music was referred to as 'Dorsey's.'"

Something Within

Words and Music by L. E. Campbell

1. Preach-ers and teach-ers would make their ap-peal, Fight-ing as sol - diers on great bat - tle - fields; When to their plead - ings my poor heart did yield, All I could

say,————— there is some-thing with - in.

Chorus
Some-thing with - in me that hold - eth the

reins, Some-thing with - in me that ban-ish - es

pain; Some-thing with - in me. I can-not ex -

plain, All that I know——— there is some-thing with-in.

2. *Have you that something, that*
burning desire?
Have you that something, that never
doth tire?
Oh, if you have it, that Heavenly
Fire!
Then let the world know there is
something within.

3. *I met God one morn', my soul*
feeling bad,
Heart heavy laden with a bowed
down head.
He lifted my burden and made me
so glad,
All that I know there is something
within.

*M*iss Lucie" Campbell authored this song in 1919. A performer, music director, composer, and teacher, Miss Lucie is considered one of the greatest influences on setting the music performance standard within the black Baptist church. This standard was set over a period of forty years by a small group of songwriters and singers, of which Miss Lucie was an integral part. Her songs gained classic status within the music published by the National Baptist Convention, U.S.A., Inc. Miss Lucie was born in Mississippi, of slave lineage, and came to be known as one of the most influential women within the Convention, the largest African-American organization in the world, having a membership of more than six million.

Miss Lucie dedicated this song to a blind singer named Connie Rosemond. Mr. Rosemond, who was quite poor, played his guitar on Beale Street in Memphis, Tennessee. One very cold, rainy winter day, Connie Rosemond stood out on Beale Street, his feet wrapped up in used burlap rags, playing hymns and spirituals as people passed by. Some local men, who had just stumbled out of a bar, asked him to play some "good ole Southern blues." They even offered to tip him five dollars, but Connie refused. Miss Lucie, who was shopping at a nearby fish market, overheard the exchange, including Mr. Rosemond's reply that he could only play songs that came from "something within." It was that comment that spurred Miss Lucie to write this song, which was eventually performed at the National Baptist Convention in 1919 by the blind street singer who had inspired it, Mr. Connie Rosemond. The writing of "Something Within" brought national recognition to songwriter Miss Lucie Campbell.

"Something Within" has long been a favorite in many churches because of its obvious reference to the Spirit of God dwelling within the believer.

It is in response to the moving of that "something within" that prompted the writing of another popular gospel selection and the title song of this book, "Ev'ry Time I Feel the Spirit."

Stand By Me

Words and Music by Charles Albert Tindley (c. 1851–1933)

1. When the storms of life are rag-ing, Stand by me (stand by me);

When the storms of life are rag-ing, Stand by me (stand by me);

When the world is toss-ing me Like a ship u-pon the sea;

Thou who rul-est wind and wa-ter, Stand by me (stand by me).

2. *In the midst of tribulations,*
   Stand by me;
   In the midst of tribulations,
   Stand by me;
   When the hosts of hell assail,
   And my strength begins to fail,
   Thou who never lost a battle,
   Stand by me.

3. *In the midst of faults and failures,*
   Stand by me;
   In the midst of faults and failures,
   Stand by me;
   When I do the best I can,
   And my friends misunderstand,
   Thou who knowest all about me,
   Stand by me.

4. *In the midst of persecution,*
   Stand by me;
   In the midst of persecution
   Stand by me;
   When my foes in battle array,
   Undertake to stop my way,
   Thou who saved Paul and Silas,
   Stand by me.

5. *When I'm growing old and feeble,*
   Stand by me;
   When I'm growing old and feeble,
   Stand by me;
   When my life becomes a burden,
   And I'm nearing chilly Jordan,
   O Thou "Lily of the Valley,"
   Stand by me.

*R*everend Charles Albert Tindley wrote "Stand By Me" in 1905. This song, along with "The Storm Is Passing Over," "Nothing Between," "Leave It There," "We'll Understand It Better By and By," and others, has become a classic of the African-American musical tradition and culture. Over and over again in many of Tindley's songs we see a recurring theme, which is the belief that it is only through struggle that we are ever truly changed. He also believed that struggle was the necessary element in finding release from the things of this world that tie us down or hold us back. In many of his songs there are references to these struggles, alluded to as "storms of life." And though Tindley speaks of the storms of life as inevitable and necessary, he also writes of the assurance of reaching the other side.

Nowhere is this theme seen more clearly than in "Stand By Me." Tindley doesn't say *if* storms come along: he says, "*When* the storms of life are raging, Stand by me." He recognized the inevitability of trials and struggles in this lifetime, and acknowledged his inability to withstand them in his own strength. Instead, he looked to God "who rulest wind and water" and "who never lost a battle" to carry him safely through to the other side. This message had great appeal to the black community, which had already weathered so many a tempest and seldom got a respite before another set in. The inevitability of battles was a lesson learned early in life for those of African-American descent. But the dependability of God in the midst of those storms was something else learned early in life—at a mother's knee, from a singing grandmother, from a preacher who "sang" his sermons, from a father who sang as he labored and toiled to find a way to support his family. Stories of hardship were passed down from generation to generation in song; but those songs also passed along a rich heritage of faith and victory in the midst of adversity.

Sweet, Sweet Spirit

Words and Music by Doris Akers

1. There's a sweet, sweet spir - it in this place,_____ And I know that it's the spir - it of__ the Lord._____

2. There are

Chorus

Sweet Ho - ly Spir - it, Sweet Heav'n - ly Dove,

Stay right here with— us Fill - ing us with— Your

love.— And for these bless - ings We lift our hearts with

praise;— With - out a doubt we'll know— that we have

been re - vived,— When— we shall leave— this place.—

2. *There are sweet expressions on each*   *And I know that it's the presence*
   face,   *of the Lord.*

*S*weet, Sweet Spirit" author Doris Akers was born in Brookfield, Missouri, in 1923. Her songwriting career began very early, at the age of ten. Over the years she has written more than three hundred songs, and is one of the best-known gospel music composers, arrangers, and performers to have gained prominence since the 1940s.

Doris, choir director for the Skypilot Church in Los Angeles, was preparing the choir for the service one Sunday morning. Just before worship service was about to begin she felt the need for the choir members to continue a little longer with her in the pre-service prayer time. She sensed the need to "pray through" for the service; in other words, to pray until they felt sure they had been heard by God and had heard from Him in return. This did not surprise the choir members, as they were used to spending time with Doris before each service, asking God to bless their music. Doris had once told them, "I feel that prayer is more important than great voices." Although they had already had their customary time of pre-service prayer, when their leader asked them to continue on, they readily agreed.

As the prayer time progressed, Doris began to wonder how she would ever be able to intervene and stop their time in prayer together so they could move on to the service. The choir had become so caught up in prayer that no one seemed ready to stop. Finally Doris announced, "We have to go. I hate to leave this room and I know you hate to leave, but you know we do have to go to the service. But there is such a sweet, sweet Spirit in this place."

It was then that the song "Sweet, Sweet Spirit" was born. Doris explains it this way: "Songwriters always have their ears open to a song. The song started 'singing' to me. I wanted to write it down, but couldn't. I thought the song would be gone after the service. Following the dismissal I went home. The next morning, to my surprise, I heard the song again, so I went to the piano and wrote it."

Take My Hand, Precious Lord

Words and Music by Thomas A. Dorsey (1899–1993)

Slowly, with spirit

Pre-cious Lord, take my hand, Lead me on, let me stand,— I am tired, I am weak, I am worn;— Through the storm, through the night, Lead me on to the light,— Take my hand,— pre-cious

Lord, ___ Lead me home. ___

1. When my way grows drear, Pre-cious Lord, lin-ger

near, ___ When my life is al - most

gone, ___ Hear my cry, hear my

call, Hold my hand lest I fall; ___ Take my

hand,— pre - cious Lord,— Lead me home._____

2. *When the darkness appears,*
   And the night draws near,
   And the day is past and gone,
   At the river I stand,

Guide my feet, hold my hand;
Take my hand, precious Lord,
Lead me home.

*T*ake My Hand, Precious Lord" is probably Thomas A. Dorsey's most famous song; it has become a classic in the field of gospel music. Sung today in many languages throughout the world, it has sold millions of copies of sheet music and records. The story of the writing of this song, in Dorsey's words, "came twisting out of my very heart" following the death of his wife and child.

It seems that Dorsey, along with a songwriter friend named E. C. Davis, was scheduled to sing at a revival meeting in another town. Dorsey's first wife, Nettie Harper, was expecting a child any day. Reluctant to leave her but feeling obligated to fulfill his commitment, he and Davis got into Dorsey's car and left Chicago for St. Louis. They had gone about thirty miles when Dorsey suddenly realized he had left his briefcase containing all his music at home. They immediately turned around and went back to Chicago. When he got into the house, Dorsey found his wife asleep and decided not to wake her. But when he climbed back into the car, his companion climbed out, explaining that he had suddenly decided not to make the trip. In spite of Dorsey's objections, Davis would not get back into the car, and so Dorsey went on to St. Louis without him.

In looking back on those two incidents—having to return for the briefcase and then his friend's sudden decision not to accompany him—Dorsey often wondered if they were signs given to prevent his going to the revival. If so, he ignored them, instead receiving a telegram at the revival meeting on the following night. His wife had died in childbirth. The Reverend Jesse Adams, a friend of Dorsey's, drove him home, as he was too upset to drive himself. When Dorsey arrived in Chicago he was not allowed to see his wife, although he did see the baby briefly. Tragically, the child also died soon after.

"All the heart for writing gospel music went out of me during those hours of grief," Dorsey said. In fact, he was tempted to give up writing gospel songs completely. Thankfully, he didn't. Instead, he went on to write what he called "the greatest song in my catalog."

Until I Found the Lord

Words and Music by Clara Ward

cried,   Un - til I found the Lord. My soul,——

I cried, yes, I cried un - til I found the Lord.

O——————— my soul,—— O———————— my soul,—

Just could-n't rest con-tent-ed,   just could-n't rest con-tent-ed,

O   Un - til   I found the Lord.

Just could-n't rest con-tent-ed un - til   I found the Lord.

2. *Lord, I moaned, yes, I moaned, . . .*   3. *Lord, I prayed, yes, I prayed, . . .*

*C*lara Ward, the author of this song, is considered one of the top names in gospel music. Clara was among the few gospel singers who did not decline offers to perform in nightclubs and theaters. Along with Della Reese, who also accepted such offers, Clara defended her position against much criticism from ministers and many within the African-American community, including other gospel performers. She explained that she was not accepting these offers in order to entertain, but rather to evangelize. Clara admitted that she realized not everyone shared her feelings on how and where to evangelize, but she stood by her belief that God had called her to take the gospel message beyond the church walls. Because of that belief, Clara, along with her group, the Clara Ward Singers, sang gospel at the Apollo Theater in New York, as well as in nightclubs in Las Vegas, and was very well received.

One of the members of the Clara Ward Singers was musical genius Marion Williams, now considered a gospel legend. Marion successfully spanned the historic and contemporary gospel scenes, influencing such singing greats as Aretha Franklin, Ruth Brown, and Little Richard. She has also shared the stage with Duke Ellington and Dizzy Gillespie. *Rolling Stone* magazine has referred to Williams as not only the greatest of all gospel singers but "possibly the best singer ever." But Marion Williams was one who refused to leave gospel to cross over to secular music. "I don't have nothing against other people and what they do," she said. "But I don't want no part of singing secular music. I was offered $100,000 to make one blues record, and I turned it down. I sing for the Lord, and that's enough for me."

Williams wasn't the only one who was offered big money to make the switch from gospel to secular. At one time Clara was offered $10,000 by Savoy Records if she would give up singing gospel and become a blues singer. This offer she firmly refused, although some gospel singers defected, bringing their style of gospel singing into various popular music styles, including rhythm and blues, soul, funk, and other contemporary forms.

Clara had a deep love of hymns and was fascinated with a type of gospel music known as the "gospel waltz," a style she incorporated into her arrangement of William Brewster's well-known song "At the Cross."

The late William Herbert Brewster of Memphis, Tennessee, a dynamic preacher and one of the most prolific gospel song composers of all time, is credited with having given Clara one of her first breaks. Brewster, who lived from 1897 to 1987 and wrote such well-known songs as "Surely God Is Able," "Lord, I've Tried," "Let Us Go Back to the Old Land Mark," "Peace Be Still," "Have Faith in God," and "Pay Day," was putting on a passion play. Clara attended and Brewster let her sing "Just a Moment in God's Presence" at the intermission. Everyone loved her. In remembering Clara, Brewster said, "She had more energy than any worm in an apple somewhere."

We'll Understand It Better By and By

Words and Music by Charles Albert Tindley (c. 1851–1933)

1. We are oft-en tossed and driv'n on the rest-less sea of time, Som-bre

skies and howl-ing tem-pests oft suc-ceed a bright sun-shine,— In that

land of per-fect day, when the mists have rolled a-way, We will

D.S.: how we're o - ver-come; For we'll

Fine (to next verse)

un - der-stand it bet-ter by and by.

un - der-stand it bet-ter by and by.

Chorus

By and by____ when the morn-ing comes, When the saints of

D.S.

God are gath-ered home, We'll tell the sto - ry

2. *We are often destitute of the things*
   that life demands,
   Want of food and want of shelter—
   thirsty hills and barren lands,
   We are trusting in the Lord, and
   according to His word,
   We will understand it better by
   and by.

3. *Trials dark on ev'ry hand, and we*
   cannot understand,
   All the ways that God would lead
   us to that blessed promised Land;

But He guides us with His eye and
we'll follow till we die.
For we'll understand it better by
and by.

4. *Temptations, hidden snares often*
   take us unawares,
   And our hearts are made to bleed for
   many a thoughtless word or deed,
   And we wonder why the test when
   we try to do our best.
   But we'll understand it better by
   and by.

*W*e'll Understand It Better By and By" was written by the Reverend Charles Albert Tindley in 1905. As in many of Tindley's compositions, we see reference to the storms of life, which Tindley, beginning with his early childhood when he was "hired out" to plantation owners, knew well. More important, though, he knew the God who calms the storms—and he wrote about Him eloquently. One of the reasons he wrote so often about the storms of life is because of his firm belief that struggles were necessary if there was to be any real and lasting change in a person's life. This belief or theme was widely accepted within the black community, being passed down through oral tradition. Regarding trials and sufferings he said, "I welcome . . . all the persecutions, unkindnesses, hard sayings and whatever God allows to come upon me. I welcome the hottest fire of trials if it is needed for my purification."

Tindley's method of writing stirred listeners and invited them to participate in the songs. He had a flair for writing a particular type of chorus known as a "sing-along" chorus. Sing-along choruses were so exciting or moving that congregations automatically joined in the singing. As a result, many of Tindley's songs are better known by the first line of the chorus than by the original title. "We'll Understand It Better By and By" is a perfect example, being known to many as "By and By When the Morning Comes."

Tindley wasn't the only songwriter known for composing these sing-along choruses. Thomas A. Dorsey also wrote them, as did James Cleveland. Cleveland, whose successful career included both gospel and secular music, was born in Chicago in 1931. Singing in church choirs as a young boy, Cleveland first received attention as a singer when he was eight years old. He sang a solo with the Chicago's Pilgrim Baptist Church choir, which was directed by Dorsey. Teaching himself to play the piano, Cleveland's career progressed as he sang with different groups and individuals through the years: the Caravans, the Gospelaires, the Roberta Martin Singers, the Meditations Singers, and even with Mahalia Jackson. His recording of "The Love of God" in 1960 won him wide recognition, and his 1962 recording of "Peace Be Still" earned him such titles as "Crown Prince of Gospel" and "King of Gospel." Cleveland was the founder of the successful Gospel Music Workshop of America and was also the first black gospel artist to receive a star on Hollywood's Walk of Fame. In addition to his successful singing career, Cleveland served for a time as pastor to the New Greater Harvest Baptist Church and founded and pastored the Cornerstone Institutional Baptist Church in Los Angeles.

"We'll Understand It Better By and By" is often referred to as a "funeral song" because of its obvious application to the pain and grief of the loss of a loved one, as well as its universal popularity at funerals.

We've Come This Far by Faith

Words and Music by Albert A. Goodson

move___ all___ mis - er - y and strife, That's why we've

2. *(optional, spoken): Just the other*
day I heard a man say he didn't
believe in God's Word;

I can say God has made a way,
He's never failed me yet,
(sung): Thank God, we've . . .

*W*ritten by Albert Goodson, "We've Come This Far by Faith" is another great choir processional, performed not only in African-American churches but in many other Christian churches. It is a triumphant song that makes both a declaration and a promise—a promise for the future based on the declaration of past performance: God has brought us through so much already; we can be sure He will continue to do so.

The fact that African-Americans have survived as a people through their torturous history is in itself a lesson in walking by faith. Individuals who have "been purified in the fire" have a strong inner sense of obligation to share their success. Singing about that faith-walk is a natural way of encouraging others to continue on in that walk. Former United Nations ambassador Dr. Alan Keyes summarized that strong sense of obligation to pass along what has been learned in his book *Masters of the Dream: The Strength and Betrayal of Black America.* He explains that the "ingredients that composed the strength of the black community" are easily recognizable in the people's backgrounds. The foundations of African-American moral identity were based on the examples and guidance of older family members, and because of these positive influences, their pride and sense of self was very real, being rooted in close role models. Although African-Americans understood and appreciated their individuality, they also developed a strong sense of community. They recognized that their words and actions influenced others. They felt a sense of responsibility to pass on the faith that had been their mainstay in both the good times and the bad. According to Keyes, this strong individualism and group empathy were "developed as instruments of everyday endurance and resistance" throughout the history of black Americans.

"We've Come This Far by Faith" is more than a song of praise to the God who has brought them safely thus far—although it most certainly is that. It is also a word of encouragement and direction to other weary travelers along the road, both present and future, a word that can best be summarized from the hymn "Amazing Grace":

'Tis grace hath brought [us] safe thus far, and grace will lead [us] home.

Yes, Lord

Words and Music by Bishop Charles H. Mason (1866–1961)

Lord, yes,— Lord, yes, Lord,— yes, Lord.—

— 1. My soul says yes,———— my soul says yes,——

— my soul says yes,———— my soul says yes,——

— my soul says yes,———— my soul says yes.

2. *Yes, to your will,* . . .   5. *We thank you, Lord,* . . .

3. *Yes, to your way,* . . .   6. *Come the more,* . . .

4. *We praise you, Lord,* . . .   7. *In my soul,* . . .

*B*ishop Charles Henry Mason of Mississippi was the author of "Yes, Lord." As mentioned earlier, Mason was the founder of the Pentecostal denomination known as the Church of God in Christ (COGIC). Along with other Pentecostal denominations, COGIC has had a powerful effect on gospel music's style. In fact, the style of congregational singing as a whole underwent great transformations due to the new Pentecostal congregations, who were known for a style of singing and worship intended to bring about a turning over of control of self from the singer to the Spirit of God. This yielding of oneself to God's Spirit was a primary ingredient of Pentecostal worship services. The type of songs most often sung during testimony or "tarrying" services within these Pentecostal denominations were sometimes called "congregational gospels." Basically this transformation of musical style took place at about the turn of the century. Songs referred to as "shout" songs became very popular in Pentecostal congregational-song services.

Not only were these songs a true departure from the Baptist or Methodist congregational styles already so popular, but they incorporated entirely new types of instrumental accompaniment. Tambourines, pianos, even a washtub bass, were introduced onto the church scene. Twentieth-century gospel found its spiritual nurturing ground in this type of music.

Bishop Mason was one of the most instrumental influences in the founding of that spiritual nurturing ground. He is renowned as having been a major force in establishing the turn-of-the-century style of African-American gospel music. In fact, the official COGIC hymnal is called *Yes, Lord! The Church of God in Christ Hymnal,* and was copyrighted in 1982, the Diamond Jubilee Year of COGIC. In the commentary on this song contained within COGIC's hymnal is the following statement: "When the saints sing, 'Yes, Lord!', we are saying 'Yes' to God's will; 'Yes' to God's way; and 'Yes' to God's direction in our lives."

III.
The Euro-American Hymns

Hymns of Watts, Wesley, Crosby, and others, 1600–1950

❦

Blessed assurance, Jesus is mine!
O what a foretaste of glory divine!
Heir of salvation, purchase of God,
Born of His Spirit, washed in His blood.

$\mathcal{S}$inging psalms and hymns and spiritual songs has been a part of Christian worship since the church's foundation soon after Christ's resurrection. The first believers met together regularly, not only to hear preaching and teaching from the Bible, but to worship God in song. In the first centuries of the church, when persecution of believers was widespread, these meetings often took place in private homes and even in caves and catacombs. The singing often consisted of reciting (usually a cappella—without musical accompaniment) an antiphonal hymn (church music sung by two groups, each responding to the other) to Christ.

Bishop Ambrose, also known as Saint Ambrose, lived from A.D. 339 to 397 and was the Roman bishop of Milan. Ambrose is credited with influencing the Roman emperor Augustine's conversion to Christianity, and was also instrumental in instituting hymn-singing in Western church services in A.D. 386. Augustine's conversion to Christianity resulted in a respite for persecuted Christians; it was during that time that the church began to meet more openly, often in large buildings or palace chapels. Gregorian chant is the liturgical chant of the Roman Catholic Church and was named after Pope Gregory I (Gregory the Great), who presided from A.D. 590–604 and was thought to have developed it. Organ music became a mainstay of church music when in 826 Charlemagne's son installed an organ in the palace chapel at Aachen. As abbots and nuns, eager to praise God in music, began to develop new songs and sounds, polyphonic music—music incorporating harmonies and multiple melodies—came to replace the Gregorian chants.

However, worshipping through song was confined to members of the clergy and choir members; the congregants themselves did not participate except as listeners. In fact, from A.D. 574 until Martin Luther's time, women were forbidden to sing in church. It was Luther, the man often credited with the start of the Protestant Reformation, who helped return the singing of hymns to the people. Having co-produced a hymnal in 1524, Luther said, "I place music next to theology and give it the highest praise."

But even with Luther's contributions, it was at least another 150 years before any real change took place in the church's music. During that time, vibrant musical expression was still sadly lacking for English-speaking believers. Dr. Isaac Watts, an English minister and physician who lived from 1674 to 1748, complained, "To see the dull indifference, the negligent and thoughtless air, that sits upon the faces of the whole assembly while the psalm is on their lips, might tempt even a charitable observer to suspect the fervour of inward religion."

It was that very observation that spurred Watts to seek a solution to such dull, lifeless singing. As a result, the modern hymn came into being. Watts gave the church a freer, more powerful means of expressing its faith and worship through the creation of such hymns as "When I Survey the Wondrous Cross," "Jesus Shall Reign," and "Joy to the World!," the last of which is included in this section. It wasn't long until Charles Wesley (1707–1788), John Newton (1725–1807), and others followed in Watts's footsteps.

The music of Dr. Watts greatly impacted the worship styles of black Christians, as did the music of the Wesley brothers—Charles and John— and many other hymn composers. Their songs brought about a new direction in church music, moving it away from psalm singing toward religious poem singing. It was this type of singing that became known as "meter singing," although it was somewhat different from the meter singing of the Great Awakening, a period of intense religious revival in America between 1720 and 1770.

Since the time of the great English composers, church music has expanded to include the singing of spirituals, gospels, and the modern praise songs that are so popular today. And yet those old English hymns, penned some 250 years ago, still hold a valuable and cherished place in the hearts of worshippers everywhere. The African-American church is no exception.

Although both the black Methodists and the black Baptists adopted Watts's hymns, it was the Baptists who "blackened" them. Taking the time signature and rhythm and virtually throwing it out, they began a new system. This innovation, begun before 1875, was based on the style of singing from the English hymns, but it was very different. The congregational singing that evolved from this change was very similar to that of the spirituals, although the original text was retained. As African-Americans took the Christian religion as their own, they also took its music, breathing new life into it and adapting it to their history, culture, and situation.

The primary way these hymns were sung in African-American churches was that the worship leader (usually the preacher or deacon) would "line out" the hymn, and the congregation would follow by singing it. Then would follow the "moaning" or humming of the stanza. This is an understandable and natural format for people who for the most part were illiterate and for whom the use of hymnals was therefore virtually nonexistent.

In 1801, Richard Allen, founding bishop of the African Methodist Episcopal (A.M.E.) Church, published a hymnal for the congregation he had established in 1794. The A.M.E. Church got its start when Allen, a licensed Methodist preacher, and other black congregants, were driven by discriminatory treatment from the prestigious St. George's Methodist Episcopal Church in Philadelphia, which they had attended and supported for years. It seems the black members were astonished when they were informed one Sunday morning that they could no longer sit in the pews they had previously used. They were ordered by the sexton to go and sit up in the balcony at the rear of the church, which they did. Then, as the prayer was offered up, a white trustee ordered one of the black church members—Absalom Jones—to move even further back. Jones pleaded with the trustee to allow him to wait until after the prayer was finished, but the trustee refused his request, enlisting another white congregant to assist him in moving Jones. As Jones knelt in prayer, he was lifted up and carried off. When the prayer ended, the entire group of black worshippers walked out of the church and, with Allen as their leader, started a new fellowship in a former blacksmith shop. It was from these humble beginnings that the worldwide A.M.E. denomination began.

Allen's hymnal, *A Collection of Spiritual Songs and Hymns Selected from Various Authors by Richard Allen, African Minister,* consisted of fifty-four hymn texts (words without tunes) drawn chiefly from the collections of Isaac Watts, Charles Wesley, John Wesley, and other writers favored by the Methodists of the period. Allen's hymnal stands as the first anthology of hymns collected for use by an African-American congregation. It was also the first hymnal to use "wandering" refrains and verses or short choruses attached at random to orthodox hymn stanzas. The practice of wandering refrains is a form of improvisation, and since improvisation was also inherent in the spirituals, here is evidence that connects the musical tastes of the slaves with people such as Richard Allen and his congregation, who were free.

It is obvious then that the singing of hymns was adopted into early African-

American worship services, and yet was adapted to fit African-Americans' particular heritage as well as the social culture of the time. The resulting style was carried down through the years of enslavement to the African-American church after Emancipation. The hymns are still very popular in black churches today, and their majesty is highly revered. A study of the history of some individual hymns and hymn writers can only serve to enhance the appreciation of these cherished songs of worship and praise.

All Hail the Power of Jesus' Name

Words by Edward Perronet (1721–1792)
Tune "Miles Lane" by William Shrubsole (1760–1806),
and tune "Coronation" by Oliver Holden (1765–1844)

1. All hail the power of Jesus' name! Let angels prostrate fall; Bring forth the royal diadem, And crown Him Lord of all; Bring forth the royal diadem, And crown Him Lord of all. Amen.

2. Ye chosen seed of Israel's race,
   Ye ransomed from the fall,
   Hail Him who saves you by His
      grace,
   And crown Him Lord of all!
   Hail Him who saves you by His
      grace,
   And crown Him Lord of all!

3. Let ev'ry kindred, ev'ry tribe,
   On this terrestrial ball,
   To Him all majesty ascribe,
   And crown Him Lord of all!
   To Him all majesty ascribe,
   And crown Him Lord of all!

4. O that with yonder sacred throng
   We at His feet may fall!
   We'll join the everlasting song,
   And crown Him Lord of all!
   We'll join the everlasting song,
   And crown Him Lord of all!

5. Sinners, whose love can ne'er forget,
   The wormwood and the gall,
   Go, spread your trophies at His feet,
   And crown Him Lord of all!
   Go, spread your trophies at His feet,
   And crown Him Lord of all!

6. Crown Him, ye martyrs of your God,
   Who from His altar call;
   Extol Him in whose path ye trod,
   And crown Him Lord of all!
   Extol Him in whose path ye trod,
   And crown Him Lord of all!

*T*his "national anthem of Christendom," a hymn of praise, was penned by Reverend Edward Perronet. Perronet's French Huguenot family fled from religious persecution in France, first to Switzerland and then later to England. Edward worked diligently in the evangelistic work of the 1740s and '50s in England with Charles and John Wesley, the famous Methodists. He later went out on his own as a pastor of a small Congregational chapel in Canterbury. His temperament inclined him to write hymns and other forms of poetry, which he published anonymously in 1785. "All Hail the Power of Jesus' Name," written in 1789, is the only one of Perronet's hymns still found in common use today.

Perronet wrote six stanzas of verse for this song. A seventh stanza was added later by John Rippon (1751–1836). This beautiful hymn is a memorial to the Resurrection of Jesus Christ. As in many eighteenth-century hymns, Perronet uses biblical imagery and phraseology throughout the verses, calling upon men of all nations and times, as well as angels, to join in the singing of praise.

There are several tunes to this wonderful text. In my father's church, at various times, I remember singing this song to three different melodies. In fact, as long as I can remember, I have sung this wonderful praise to the name of Jesus. The tune I like best and sing most often is "Coronation," written in 1793 by Oliver Holden, a self-taught musician of Charlestown, Massachusetts. I can recall singing it one time with the congregation—and, I believe, with the choirs of heaven's angels—when I literally sensed the glorious presence of the Lord Jesus Christ Himself, walking in the procession before me. For a moment I could almost imagine what it must feel like if, for example, the king or queen of England rode by in the royal carriage—only this seemed even more majestic.

Sung in the black church as well as the white over many years, "All Hail the Power of Jesus' Name" is a song of great dignity and awe.

Amazing Grace

Words by John Newton (1725–1807) (verses 1–4),
John P. Rees (1828–1900) (verse 5)
Tune: "American melody from Carrel & Clayton's
Virginia Harmony, 1831"

once— was— lost, but now— am— found, was

blind, but— now I see.—

2. 'Twas grace that taught my heart
    to fear, and grace my fears
    relieved;
   How precious did that grace appear
    the hour I first believed!

3. Through many dangers, toils and
    snares I have already come;
   'Tis grace hath brought me safe
    thus far, and grace will lead me
    home.

4. The Lord has promised good to me;
    His word my hope secures;
   He will my shield and portion be
    as long as life endures.

5. Yes, when this flesh and heart
    shall fail, and mortal life shall
    cease;
   I shall possess, within the veil, a
    life of joy and peace.

6. The earth shall soon dissolve like
    snow, the sun forbear to shine;
   But God, who called me here
    below, will be forever mine.

7. When we've been there ten
    thousand years, bright shining
    as the sun,
   We've no less days to sing God's
    praise than when we'd first
    begun.

Calling himself a "wretch" who was lost and blind, John Newton, the author of this hymn, recalled leaving school at the age of eleven to begin life as a rough, debauched seaman. Eventually he engaged in the despicable practice of capturing people from West Africa to be sold as slaves to markets around the world. But one day the grace of God put fear into the heart of this wicked slave trader through a fierce storm. Greatly alarmed and fearful of a shipwreck, Newton began to read *The Imitation of Christ* by Thomas à Kempis. God used this book to lead Newton to a genuine conversion and a dramatic change in his way of life.

Feeling a definite call to study for the ministry, Newton was encouraged and greatly influenced by John and Charles Wesley and George Whitefield. At the age of thirty-nine, John Newton became an ordained minister of the Anglican Church at the little village of Olney, near Cambridge, England. To add further impact to his powerful preaching, Newton introduced simple heartfelt hymns rather than the usual psalms in his services. When not enough hymns could be found, Newton began to write his own, often assisted by his close friend William Cowper. In 1779 their combined efforts produced the famous *Olney Hymns* hymnal. "Amazing Grace" is from that collection.

Until the time of his death at the age of eighty-two, John Newton never ceased to marvel at the grace of God that had transformed him so completely. Shortly before his death he is quoted as proclaiming with a loud voice during a message, "My memory is nearly gone, but I remember two things: That I am a great sinner and that Christ is a great Savior!"

When I asked my eighty-four-year-old Aunt Lillie what this song means to her, she rose up in her seat and said, "Oh, I get a sense of security. I feel like I can go on. Just thinking about the grace of God gives me a push, gives me strength, when I think of how He has kept me over these years, and that He'll keep on keeping me. Oh, it's a powerful song, and I can hear it all the time."

Ninety-four-year-old Grandma Johnnie, sitting in her apartment in Princeton, exclaimed, "Oh, oh, oh, oh! Every time I hear it, I feel so good. I can remember many years ago, down in South Carolina, we'd be in prayer meeting. Sometimes you'd be feeling a little sad and down and you'd begin to hear somebody from somewhere within the church begin softly to sing, 'Amazing Grace, how sweet the sound,' and you'd begin to feel the Lord lifting you up and bringing joy to your soul. Oh, oh, oh, oh!"

Battle Hymn of the Republic

Words by Julia Ward Howe (1819–1910)
Music by William Steffe

1. Mine eyes have seen the glo-ry of the com-ing of the Lord, He is

tram-pling out the vin-tage where the grapes of wrath are stored; He hath

loosed the fate-ful light-ning of His ter-ri-ble swift sword— His

truth is march-ing on.

Chorus

Glo - ry! glo - ry, hal - le - lu - jah! Glo - ry! glo - ry, hal - le-

lu - jah! Glo - ry! glo - ry, hal - le-

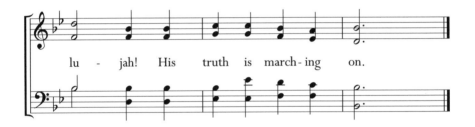

lu - jah! His truth is march-ing on.

2. I have seen Him in the watchfires
  of a hundred circling camps,
They have builded Him an altar in
  the evening dews and damps;
I can read His righteous sentence
  by the dim and flaring lamps—
His day is marching on.

3. He has sounded forth the trumpet
  that shall never sound retreat,
He is sifting out the hearts of men
  before His judgment seat;

O be swift, my soul, to answer
  Him! be jubilant, my feet!
Our God is marching on.

4. In the beauty of the lilies Christ
  was born across the sea,
With a glory in His bosom that
  transfigures you and me;
As He died to make men holy, let
  us die to make men free,
While God is marching on.

*T*he author of this powerful hymn was Julia Ward Howe, a New Yorker of the upper class. Julia was married to a Boston physician who worked principally with the mentally handicapped. He was also a passionate abolitionist who helped another abolitionist, the well-known John Brown. It was this John Brown the soldiers sang about whose plan it was to set up a stronghold of liberated slaves in the mountains. Brown was hanged for murder and treason in Charleston, Virginia (now part of West Virginia), before he could follow through on his plan.

Julia and her husband went out to visit the Union army in Potomac, Maryland, near Washington one afternoon in November 1861. As they spent the night with the troops, who were singing their song about John Brown, James Freeman Clarke, a friend of the Howes, suggested to Julia that she write new words for the tune. Clarke had left the Unitarians to found his own Church of the Disciples in Boston. Julia considered his suggestion as they sat under the canvas tents that evening. Early the next morning she got up and lit a candle. "In the dimness with the old stump of a pen which I remembered to have used the day before, I scrawled the verses almost without looking at the paper," Julia said.

As is evident in prior church history, quite a number of hymns were set to secular tunes, the "Battle Hymn of the Republic" being one of them. In explaining her reason for having followed through on her friend's suggestion to write new words to the tune, Julia said that upon hearing, "John Brown's body lies a-molding in the grave," she felt that "such a good tune deserved rather more uplifting words." Actually, the song, before being sung as "John Brown's Body," was originally a Methodist hymn. Julia simply returned the tune to its original purpose. "Mine eyes have seen the glory" was published for the first time in the *Atlantic Monthly* of February 1862. It was there that it was given its present title. Julia Howe received four dollars in return for all her rights to the piece. The hymn went on to become one of the North's major marching songs during the Civil War. When it is sung today, the third line of the fifth verse is often changed to "As he died to make men holy, let us live to make men free."

My grandmother, Emma Evaline Griffin Sims, told the story of how she and her grandmother, an African and once a slave, stood one day at the fence alongside the road in front of their wooden shack, waving the Union soldiers on as they rode by declaring, "War is over! The North won! The slaves are free!" Christians that they were, the two gave thanks to God for His great mercy. They were thrilled that God had prevailed in justice on their behalf.

Grandmother eventually died in her bedroom next to mine in our house in Atlantic City, New Jersey. I don't remember hearing any struggles or difficulties during that night, nor did I hear anyone saying there were such. I believe she just breathed in the mercies of God, breathed out His precious name—Jesus—one last time, and was ushered into His presence by the angels. She was truly free at last, free at last, thank God A-mighty, free at last!

Blessed Assurance

Words by Fanny J. Crosby (1820–1915)
Music by Phoebe P. Knapp

God,— Born of His Spir - it, washed in His blood.—

Chorus

This is my sto - ry, this is my song,— Prais-ing my

Sav - ior all the day long;— This is my sto - ry, this is my

song,— Prais-ing my Sav - ior all the day long.—

2. *Perfect submission, perfect delight!*
   Visions of rapture now burst on my
      sight;
   Angels descending bring from above
   Echoes of mercy, whispers of love.

3. *Perfect submission—all is at rest,*
   I in my Savior am happy and blest;
   Watching and waiting, looking
      above,
   Filled with His goodness, lost in
      His love.

*T*he author of this hymn, Mrs. Frances Jane van Alstyne, who lived from 1820 until 1915, is better known by her maiden name, Fanny Crosby. Fanny was undoubtedly one of the most prolific and dearly beloved hymn writers of all time. Born in New York, Fanny was blind from infancy. When she was fourteen she attended the first special school of the blind established in the United States. As an adult she taught at that very same school, and it was there that she met her future husband, also a blind teacher.

From an early age, Fanny was writing verse. William Cullen Bryant, the distinguished American poet and hymn writer, recognized her talent and encouraged her to continue writing. Her first book of verse, *The Blind Girl and Other Poems,* was published when she was twenty-four.

It was during the singing of Isaac Watts's hymn "Here, Lord, I Give Myself Away" at a Methodist church meeting in New York that Fanny Crosby was converted to Christianity. Ira D. Sankey, the great evangelist and composer whom she met sometime later, set many of her verses to music.

Through the years, Fanny wrote more than 8,000 hymns and sacred songs, using 216 different pen names. "To God Be the Glory" is one of her most popular hymns, as are "Safe in the Arms of Jesus," "Rescue the Perishing," "I Am Thine, O Lord; I Have Heard Thy Voice," and "O My Saviour Hear Me." Although no one would claim her hymns—including "Blessed Assurance"—to be great poetry, they express the heart of the Christian gospel of salvation in a simple, moving manner. "Blessed Assurance" has for years been popular in evangelical circles, even becoming the theme song of the Billy Graham evangelistic movement, being used in his "Hour of Decision" broadcasts.

Mrs. Phoebe Knapp (1839–1908) wrote the tune for "Blessed Assurance." Phoebe was married to J. F. Knapp, founder of the Metropolitan Life Insurance Company of New York and one of the richest men in the city. There is some speculation that the tune was written before the words, since it is supposed that Mrs. Knapp toured the blind school where Fanny taught, and played the tune, which Fanny overheard and is said to almost instantly have come up with the words for.

How I love this song—and how well I remember it! It seems I grew up with it, hearing it at least once every week, either at the Sunday morning or evening service, during testimony time, or at the weekly prayer service. And each time I heard it, it was fresh, building within me a joy and confi-

dence in God—as it has done for so many through the years. Along with
"Leaning on the Everlasting Arms" and "What a Friend We Have in Jesus,"
both included in this section, "Blessed Assurance" has always been a
favorite of those who had little in the way of possessions on this earth. Just
looking ahead to the assurance of better things to come kept a continual
song of praise in their hearts and on their lips!

Come, Thou Fount

Words by Robert Robinson (1735–1790)
Music by John Wyeth (1770–1858)—(Nettleton tune)

1. Come, Thou Fount of ev - 'ry bless - ing, Tune my
heart to sing Thy grace; Streams of mer - cy, nev - er
ceas - ing, Call for songs of loud-est praise. Teach me—

some me - lo - dious son - net, Sung by— flam - ing tongues a -

bove;   Praise the   mount! O   fix me   on   it,   Mount of

God's   re - deem - ing   love.   A -   men.

2. Here I raise mine Ebenezer;
   Hither by Thy help I'm come;
   And I hope, by Thy good pleasure,
   Safely to arrive at home.
   Jesus sought me when a stranger,
   Wand'ring from the fold of God;
   He, to rescue me from danger,
   Interposed His precious blood.

3. O, to grace how great a debtor
   Daily I'm constrained to be!
   Let Thy grace, Lord, like a fetter,
   Bind my wand'ring heart to Thee.
   Prone to wander, Lord, I feel it,
   Prone to leave the God I love;
   Here's my heart, Lord, take and
     seal it,
   Seal it for Thy courts above.

*R*obert Robinson, the author of "Come, Thou Fount," grew up in London, associating with a notorious gang of hoodlums and leading a life of debauchery. Then, when he was seventeen, he attended a meeting where the noted evangelist George Whitefield was preaching. Robinson's purpose for attending the meeting was to scoff "at those poor, deluded Methodists"; however, that isn't at all how the evening turned out. By the end of the service, Robinson had responded to the altar call and professed faith in Christ as his Savior. Before long he felt that he was called to preach the gospel, and soon became the pastor of a rather large Baptist church in Cambridge, England.

Despite his questionable past and his young age, Robert Robinson became known as a proficient minister and scholar. He wrote several theological books, as well as hymns, including the words to "Come, Thou Fount," which he wrote when he was just twenty-three years old.

The words to this song show the depth of Robinson's commitment and his understanding of the necessity of God's grace in his life. This is especially evident in the third stanza, where he declares how great a debt he owed to God's grace in saving him: "O to grace how great a debtor." He also recognized that God's grace not only saved him, but also kept him from going back to his old life: "Prone to wander, Lord, I feel it, Prone to leave the God I love." He put his life completely in God's keeping with the final lines: "Here's my heart, Lord, take and seal it, Seal it for Thy courts above."

The word "Ebenezer," found in the second verse, is unfamiliar to many, but it simply means "a memorial to God's faithfulness." As is true in the other songs throughout this book, "Come, Thou Fount" was written as just such a memorial.

Great Is Thy Faithfulness

Words by Thomas O. Chisholm (1866–1960)
Music by William M. Runyan (1870–1957)

1. Great is Thy faith - ful - ness, O God my Fa - ther,
There is no shad - ow of turn - ing with Thee;
Thou chang - est not, Thy com - pas - sions, they fail not,
As Thou hast been Thou for - ev - er wilt be.

2. *Summer and winter, and springtime*
   and harvest,
   Sun, moon and stars in their
   courses above,
   Join with all nature in manifold
   witness,
   To Thy great faithfulness, mercy
   and love.

3. *Pardon for sin and a peace that*
   endureth,
   Thine own dear presence to cheer
   and to guide;
   Strength for today and bright hope
   for tomorrow,
   Blessings all mine, with ten
   thousand beside!

*A*s we see in reading through this book, many hymns were written as a result of one particular dramatic experience. "Great Is Thy Faithfulness," by Thomas Chisholm, is not that sort of hymn. It is, instead, a hymn that was written as the result of a long walk with God, one where the author saw God's faithfulness "morning by morning." Shortly before his death in 1960, Thomas Chisholm wrote that his income had been meager throughout his life because of ill-health. Yet he spoke of God's faithfulness through the years when he said, "He has given me many wonderful displays of His providing care which have filled me with astonishing gratefulness."

Born in a crude log cabin in Simpson County, Kentucky, on July 29, 1866, Thomas Obediah Chisholm came from very humble beginnings. Without ever having attended high school or obtained any other advanced education, he somehow landed a position as a schoolteacher at the age of sixteen. He taught at the same little country school he had attended in his elementary years. Then, at the age of twenty-one, Thomas got a job as associate editor of a Kentucky newspaper in Franklin County, opening up an opportunity for him to write. While working at this paper he met an evangelist, Dr. H. C. Morrison, who led him to Christ. From that moment on, Chisholm dedicated his life to serving God. Morrison then invited him to be office editor of the *Pentecostal Herald* in Louisville. Within three years of accepting that position, Chisholm's health broke down. Afterwards he worked for a time as an insurance salesman and also as a traveling evangelist, but continuing ill-health forced him to limit his work to selling insurance and writing.

Thirty years after his conversion, Chisholm was living in New Jersey, sending his poetry to a Methodist pastor-composer named Dr. William M. Runyon, also a New Jersey resident. Dr. Runyon was so impressed with Chisholm's poem "Great Is Thy Faithfulness" that he put it to music. The timeless popularity of this great hymn can be attributed in part to its being sung so often by George Beverly Shea and the choirs of the Billy Graham Crusades around the world.

His Eye Is on the Sparrow

Words by Mrs. C. D. Martin (1869–1948)
Music by Charles H. Gabriel (1856–1932)

Unison

1. Why should I feel dis - cour-aged, Why should the shad - ows come, Why should my heart be lone - ly And long for heaven and home, When Je - sus is my por - tion? My con - stant friend is He: His

2. "Let not your heart be troubled,"
   His tender word I hear,
   And resting on His goodness,
   I lose my doubts and fears;
   Tho' by the path He leadeth

But one step I may see:
His eye is on the sparrow,
And I know He watches me;
His eye is on the sparrow,
And I know He watches me.

3. *Whenever I am tempted,*
   Whenever clouds arise,
   When song gives place to sighing,
   When hope within me dies,
   I draw the closer to Him,

From care He sets me free:
His eye is on the sparrow,
And I know He watches me;
His eye is on the sparrow,
And I know He watches me.

*T*he author of "His Eye Is on the Sparrow," Mrs. Civilla Martin, was inspired to write the text to this song after a visit to a dear friend who was ill. Mrs. Martin's friend was so physically weakened by her condition that she was bedridden, yet she was never discouraged. "How can I be discouraged," she commented to Civilla, "when my heavenly Father watches over each little sparrow and I know He loves and cares for me." Her friend's words so affected Mrs. Martin that she couldn't stop thinking about them during the thirty-five-mile journey home. As soon as she arrived, she sat down and wrote the words to this inspirational hymn, which has been a source of encouragement to countless of God's people through the years.

It was Charles H. Gabriel, another famous songwriter, who eventually set Mrs. Martin's beautiful poem to music. "His Eye Is on the Sparrow" has become famous, in large part, due to the inspiring singing of Ethel Waters, who sang of God's faithfulness during the Billy Graham Crusades and on national television.

The concept of God's "eye on the sparrow" is taken from Matthew 10:29–31:

> Not even a sparrow, worth only half a penny, can fall to the ground without your Father knowing it. And the very hairs on your head are all numbered. So don't be afraid; you are more valuable to him than a whole flock of sparrows.

In looking at the Bible passage in Matthew, it is significant to me that the sparrow is used for illustration of God's care. The sparrow is the most common of all birds—not rare at all—and yet if God cares for each of the sparrows, isn't it even more believable that He cares about everything that pertains to each one of us?

Holy, Holy, Holy

Words by Reginald Heber (1783–1826)
Music by John B. Dykes (1823–1876)

1. Ho - ly, Ho - ly, Ho - ly!— Lord— God Al - might - y!

Ear - ly in the morn - ing our song shall rise to Thee;

Ho - ly, Ho - ly Ho - ly!— Mer - ci - ful and might - y!

God— in three per - sons,— bless - ed Trin - i - ty! A - men.

2. *Holy, Holy, Holy! All the saints
    adore Thee,
    Casting down their golden crowns
    around the glassy sea;
    Cherubim and seraphim falling
    down before Thee,
    Which wert and art and evermore
    shall be.*

3. *Holy, Holy, Holy! Though the
    darkness hide Thee,
    Though the eye of sinful man
    Thy glory may not see;*

*Only Thou art holy—there is none
    beside Thee,
    Perfect in pow'r, in love and
    purity.*

4. *Holy, Holy, Holy, Lord God
    Almighty!
    All Thy works shall praise Thy
    name in earth and sky and sea;
    Holy, Holy, Holy! Merciful and
    Mighty!
    God in three persons, blessed
    Trinity!*

*H*oly, Holy, Holy," written by Reginald Heber, is regarded by many—including the great Victorian poet Alfred, Lord Tennyson—as the finest hymn in the English language. Probably more than any other hymn, this great song takes the complex Christian doctrine of the Trinity and expresses it with beauty and simplicity.

Heber wrote this hymn while serving as vicar of Hodnet in Shropshire, England. He served in this capacity for the solemn days, the feast days, and the ordinary Sundays in the Church of England calendar. Heber wrote "Holy, Holy, Holy" to be sung at Hodnet on Trinity Sunday, which occurs eight weeks after Easter. This particular festival is dedicated to the Trinity—the theological doctrine of God as existing in three Persons: Father, Son, and Holy Spirit.

This hymn was first published in *A Selection of Psalms and Hymns for the Church of Banbury* shortly after Heber's death. Although originally written to be sung on a particular Sunday morning, "Holy, Holy, Holy" is sung in churches throughout the world, throughout the year, in morning and evening services, its popularity never waning.

In all, Heber wrote fifty-seven hymns, many in observance of the church calendar. In fact, he wrote one for almost every Sunday and special observance day in the church.

The tune to which "Holy, Holy, Holy" is most often sung today was written in 1861 by the Reverend John Bacchus Dykes for the original edition of *Hymns Ancient and Modern.* Although it is similar to the German tune "Wachet Auf," Heber's inspiration for the tune was probably "Trinity," by John Hopkins, to which Heber's hymn was set in 1850.

Another famous hymn on the subject of the Trinity is "Doxology," written by an Anglican bishop named Thomas Ken (1637–1711). During the years I was growing up in my father's church, I cannot recall a Sunday when we did not sing this beautiful song:

> *Praise God, from whom all blessings flow;*
> *Praise Him, all creatures here below;*
> *Praise Him above, ye heav'nly host;*
> *Praise Father, Son, and Holy Ghost.*
> *Amen.*

There are still some churches today who make it a practice to sing this hymn every week. I applaud that practice. But I would also encourage the singers to think of "Doxology" as more than a hymn that marks a certain place in the weekly service. It is an offering of praise to God for the many blessings so faithfully bestowed on us throughout our lives and throughout the lives of our ancestors.

How Great Thou Art

Words by Carl Boberg (1859–1940), translated by Stuart K. Hine
Swedish Melody

1. O Lord my God, when I in awe-some won-der___ Con-sid-er

all the worlds Thy hands have made, — I see the stars, I hear the roll-ing

thun-der, — Thy pow'r through-out the un-i-verse dis-played! —

Chorus

Then sings my soul, my Sav - ior God, to

Thee;_____ How great Thou art,_____ how great Thou

art!_____ Then sings my soul, my Sav - ior God, to

Thee; ——— How great Thou art, ——— how great Thou art! ———

2. When through the woods and forest
     glades I wander
   And hear the birds sing sweetly in
     the trees,
   When I look down from lofty
     mountain grandeur
   And hear the brook and feel the
     gentle breeze.

3. And when I think that God, His
     Son not sparing,
   Sent Him to die, I scarce can take
     it in—

That on the cross, my burden
  gladly bearing,
He bled and died to take away my
  sin!

4. When Christ shall come with shout
     of acclamation
   And take me home, what joy shall
     fill my heart!
   Then I shall bow in humble
     adoration
   And there proclaim, my God, how
     great Thou art!

*I*t is not difficult for me to relate to Carl Boberg, the author of the original Swedish poem on which "How Great Thou Art" is based. I was in
Canada during the summer of 1994, in the mountains in Banff, trying my
hand at sketching the scenery. Overwhelmed by the majesty of God's creation, I realized that even if I were the greatest artist in the world, with
the finest paints and canvas, I could not do it justice.

I imagine that is how Boberg must have felt when he first penned those
inspiring words in 1886. He had been visiting a beautiful country estate
when he was caught in a sudden thunderstorm. The storm, with its awe-
some display of thunder and lightning, didn't last long. When it was over,
the clear, brilliant sunshine burst through and the peaceful, sweet singing
of the birds resumed in the trees. Boberg fell to his knees in awe and adoration of God, then proceeded to write nine stanzas of praise. Before long,
Swedish congregations had begun to sing Boberg's poem to the melody of

an old folk tune. Stuart Hine, an English missionary, first heard the song in Russia some forty years later. Boberg's original stanzas had been translated into Russian by I. S. Prokhanoff, one of the prominent figures in the Russian evangelical movement just after the turn of the century. Hine eventually translated the verses into English, changing them somewhat from the original, while maintaining the author's intent.

Not only is this magnificent hymn a song of God's majesty, but the final stanza is a verse about going home. Hine wrote this final verse when he went home to Britain in 1948, the same year that more than 100,000 refugees from Russia and other parts of Eastern Europe poured into the United Kingdom. These refugees were all consumed with the desire to know when they were going home. When Hine wrote about this particular verse, he said, "What better message for the homeless than that of the One who went to prepare a place for the 'displaced,' of the God who invites into His own home those who will come to him through Christ."

How often that same question—"When are we going home?"—must have run through the minds of those early African slaves. Many had been abducted during the night, and carried, in bonds and chains, into the dark holes of ships, not knowing what had happened to them, where they were going, whether they would ever see their homes and families again. It is not difficult to see why this beloved hymn quickly became a favorite among African-American worshippers.

I Need Thee Every Hour

Words by Annie S. Hawks (1835–1918)
Music by Robert Lowry (1826–1899)

ten - der voice like Thine   Can   peace— af - ford.

Chorus

I need Thee, O, I need Thee,   Ev - 'ry hour I need Thee! O

bless me now, my Sav-ior, I   come— to Thee!   A - men.

2. *I need Thee ev'ry hour,*
   Stay Thou near by;
   Temptations lose their pow'r
   When Thou art nigh.

3. *I need Thee ev'ry hour,*
   In joy or pain;

Come quickly and abide,
Or life is vain.

4. *I need Thee ev'ry hour,*
   Most Holy One;
   Oh, make me Thine indeed,
   Thou blessed Son!

*A*nnie S. Hawks was the author of this great hymn. She was also a busy housewife and mother who had no idea that she was doing anything more than simply writing a deeply personal poem from her heart. Through the years, however, her hastily written words have brought spiritual strength to many—including herself. Annie told the story about the writing of her poem in 1872. It seems that one day, as a thirty-seven-year-old wife and mother, she was busy with her usual household tasks. All of a sudden she was overwhelmed with a sense of God's presence, and she found herself wondering how anyone could possibly live without Him, regardless of their circumstances. It was then, she said, that "the words were ushered into my mind and these thoughts took full possession of me."

Sixteen years after the writing of this hymn, Annie's husband died. Some time later she explained that although she did not at first understand why this hymn had so greatly touched so many people, she soon learned the reason. In experiencing her own loss, she also began to know the peace and comfort of the words God had given her to write sixteen years earlier.

So many of our favorite gospels, spirituals, and hymns were born out of a time of trial and tragedy for their authors. "I Need Thee Every Hour" was not one of those. It was instead penned in a time of security and happiness, only to be used by God to minister to the author herself when sorrow later came her way. These wonderful hymns, some of them composed more than two hundred years ago, are still bringing comfort and peace to singers and listeners today.

It Is Well with My Soul

Words by Horace G. Spafford (1828–1888)
Music by Philip Bliss (1838–1876)

1.When peace like a— ri - ver at - tend - eth my

way. When sor - rows like sea bil - lows roll, What-

ev - er my lot, Thou hast taught me to say, It is—

well, it is well with my soul.

Chorus

It is well_____ with my soul,_____
(It is well)   (with my

____ It is well, it is well with my soul.
soul)

2. *Though Satan should buffet,*
   though trials should come,
   Let this blest assurance control,
   That Christ hath regarded my
      helpless estate
   And hath shed His own blood for
      my soul!

3. *My sin—oh, the bliss of this*
      glorious thought—
   My sin not in part, but the whole,
   Is nailed to the cross, and I bear it

no more,
Praise the Lord, Praise the Lord,
   O my soul!

4. *And Lord, haste the day when my*
      faith shall be sight,
   The clouds be rolled back as a
      scroll:
   The trump shall resound and the
      Lord shall descend,
   "Even so," it is well with my soul.

*H*oratio Spafford, the author of this song, had known peaceful and happy days as a successful attorney in Chicago. He was the father of five children, an active member of a Presbyterian church, and a loyal friend and supporter of D. L. Moody and other evangelical leaders of his day. Then, without warning, a series of terrible events occurred. First there was the sudden death of the Spaffords' only son. Then, a short time later, the great Chicago fire of 1871 wiped out the family's extensive real estate investments. When Moody and his music associate, Ira Sankey, left for Great Britain for an evangelistic campaign, Spafford decided to take his family to Europe to lift their spirits and also to assist in the meetings.

In November 1873, Spafford was detained by urgent business, but he sent his wife and four daughters as scheduled on the SS *Ville du Havre,* planning to join them soon. Halfway across the Atlantic the ship was struck by an English vessel and sank in twelve minutes. All four of the Spafford daughters—Tanetta, Maggie, Annie, and Bessie—were among the 226 who drowned. Mrs. Spafford was one of the few who was miraculously saved.

Horatio Spafford stood hour after hour on the deck of the ship carrying him to rejoin his sorrowing wife in Cardiff, Wales. When the ship passed the approximate place where his precious daughters had drowned, Spafford received a strong sense of comfort from God that enabled him to write, "When sorrows like sea billows roll . . . It is well with my soul."

The morning we received the news of the death of my husband, Jim, I was in my office preparing for Sunday morning's worship service.

Immediately upon being told of his sudden death, I sensed the grace of God flooding through me. All I could say at the moment was, "Praise the Lord, for He is good and His mercy endures forever." As I continued to proceed with the service, I looked at the selection of songs I had prayerfully planned to sing for that morning. On that list was "It Is Well with My Soul."

I knew this was no time to back down or to question God. Although the children and I had not seen Jim for almost eight years—much of that time not even knowing where he was—now, facing this final resolution of our lives together, I, like Spafford, was able to say, "It is well with my soul."

Jesus, Lover of My Soul

Words by Charles Wesley (1707–1788)
Music by Simeon B. Marsh

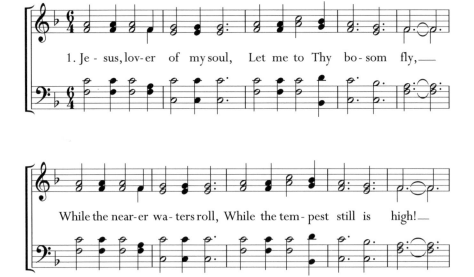

1. Je - sus, lov-er of my soul, Let me to Thy bo-som fly,—

While the near-er wa-ters roll, While the tem-pest still is high!—

Hide me, O my Sav-ior, hide,____ Till the storm of
life is past;____ Safe in-to the hav-en guide,
O re-ceive my soul at last!____ A - men.

2. Other refuge have I none—
Hangs my helpless soul on Thee;
Leave, ah, leave me not alone,
Still support and comfort me!
All my trust on Thee is stayed—
All my help from thee I bring;
Cover my defenseless head
With the shadow of Thy wing.

3. Wilt Thou not regard my call?
Wilt Thou not accept my prayer?
Lo! I sink, I faint, I fall!
Lo, on Thee I cast my care!
Reach me out Thy gracious hand!
While I of Thy strength receive,
Hoping against hope I stand,
Dying, and behold I live.

4. Thou, O Christ, art all I want,
More than all in Thee I find;
Raise the fallen, cheer the faint,
Heal the sick and lead the blind.
Just and holy is Thy name—
I am all unrighteousness;
False and full of sin I am,
Thou art full of truth and grace.

5. Plenteous grace with Thee is found,
Grace to cover all my sin;
Let the healing streams abound,
Make and keep me pure within.
Thou of life the fountain art—
Freely let me take of Thee;
Spring Thou up within my heart,
Rise to all eternity.

*T*here are various accounts of Charles Wesley's writing of this hymn, which is dated sometime around 1740. The song is an obvious prayer for God's protection, and acknowledges the author's helplessness apart from Christ. Some say the song was written after Wesley had a narrow escape from death during a storm while crossing the Atlantic. Others say he was inspired when a small bird, apparently seeking safety and protection from a predator, flew in an open window near where Wesley sat at his desk. Still others maintain that it depicts Wesley's life as a young man struggling to find peace with God prior to his dramatic Aldersgate conversion experience. But Ira Sankey, in his book *My Life and Sacred Songs,* claims that Wesley wrote the hymn when he was involved in an open-air preaching tour. During that tour he was attacked by a gang in County Down, Ireland, because they didn't like his doctrines. Wesley hid in a farmhouse. The gang followed him to the farmhouse door, but Wesley escaped through a rear window and hid under a hedge. While underneath the hedge, listening to the angry cries of the mob, he wrote this hymn.

Whichever—if any—of these accounts is accurate, "Jesus, Lover of My Soul" is one of the greatest and best-loved of Wesley's songs. But it was not without its critics. Charles's brother John omitted it from his Methodist collection of hymns in 1780. W. E. Gladstone, the great liberal statesman, commented, "It has no unity, no cohesion, no precession, and no special force." There have even been objections to the first line of the last verse, which pertains to God's grace. Perhaps that is due to a concern that the concept of the abundance of God's grace—enough to cover *all* sin—gives license to sin, rather than liberty to serve. Obviously Wesley did not perceive God's grace in that manner.

In spite of its critics, this hymn also has its admirers. Dr. George Duffield, author of "Stand Up! Stand Up for Jesus," referred to this song as "the hymn of the ages." The great nineteenth-century American theologian Henry Ward Beecher said that he would rather have written this particular hymn than to have received all the fame and glory of all the kings that ever lived. He declared that this hymn "will go on singing until the trump brings forth the angel band; and then I think it will mount up on some lip to the very presence of God."

Jesus Loves Me

Words by Anna B. Warner (1820–1915)
Music by William B. Bradbury (1816–1868)

1. Je-sus loves me! this I know, For the Bi-ble tells me so; Lit-tle ones to Him be-long; They are weak but He is strong.

Chorus

Yes, Je-sus loves me! Yes, Je-sus loves me! Yes, Je-sus loves me! The Bi-ble tells me so.

2. Jesus loves me! loves me still,
   Though I'm very weak and ill;
   That I might from sin be free,
   Bled and died upon the tree.

3. Jesus loves me! He who died
   Heaven's gate to open wide;

He will wash away my sin,
Let His little child come in.

4. Jesus loves me! He will stay
   Close beside me all the way.
   Thou hast bled and died for me;
   I will henceforth live for Thee.

*J*esus Loves Me" was written in 1860 by Anna B. Warner, who was born in West Point, New York, in 1820. Anna wrote this—and several other stories and songs—in collaboration with her sister, Susan or Susanne. The composer of the music, William Bradbury, is considered to have been one of the leading developers of early gospel music in America. He wrote many sacred songs and compiled fifty-nine books of them, which have sold more than two million copies. He was also recognized as one of the pioneers in children's music, affecting both the church and the public schools. Bradbury composed the music for Anna Warner's verses in 1861, adding the chorus to her four stanzas. The following year, "Jesus Loves Me" appeared in Bradbury's hymnal *The Golden Sower.*

Grandma Johnnie—known as "Miss Johnnie" to some—listed this song among her favorites. One day when she was ninety-six, some of us were sitting around the table with her as she shared her stories about the old days. One of those stories was about her first run-in as a young child with a mob of angry white men with "somethin' on over their faces." I couldn't help but smile as she summed up her stories. "Jesus loves me, this I know," she said simply. "Oh yes, I love that song. We sang it all the time. It was one of our favorites. You know, we sang a lot of the same songs over and over all the time 'cause some of the people couldn't read, so they sang the songs they knew and had memorized." Miss Johnnie shared a lot of tales of woe and worry, fret and fear, but in the midst of it all, she knew she was safe because she was loved by God.

One of my favorite stories is about a brilliant professor at Princeton Seminary who repeated the same words to his graduation class each year. He told them that there were still many things he did not know or understand, both in the world and in the Bible. But there was one thing he knew absolutely: "Jesus loves me, this I know, for the Bible tells me so." Knowing that, he told them, was sufficient.

I doubt there has ever been a song written that has been sung by more children throughout the world than this one. In fact, it is still one of the first songs taught to new converts in many parts of the world today.

Joy to the World!

Words from Psalm 98, adapted by Isaac Watts (1674–1748)
Music, "Antioch," arranged from George Frideric Handel (1685–1759)

1. Joy to the world! the Lord is come! Let earth re-

ceive her King, Let ev-'ry— heart—— pre-pare— Him—

room,— And heav'n and na-ture— sing, And— heav'n and na-ture—

(And heav'n and na-ture sing, And

sing, And— heav'n— and heav'n—— and na-ture— sing.

heav'n and na-ture sing–)

2. *Joy to the earth! the Savior reigns!*
   Let men their songs employ;
   While fields and floods, rocks, hills
       and plains
   Repeat the sounding joy,
   Repeat the sounding joy,
   Repeat, repeat the sounding joy.

3. *No more let sin and sorrows grow,*
   Nor thorns infest the ground;
   He comes to make His blessings flow

Far as the curse is found,
Far as the curse is found,
Far as, far as the curse is found.

4. *He rules the world with truth and*
       grace,
   And makes the nations prove
   The glories of His righteousness,
   And wonders of His love,
   And wonders of His love,
   And wonders, wonders of His love.

But the angel said to them, "Do not be afraid. I bring you good news of great joy that will be for all the people."

—Luke 2:10

*H*ow aptly named is this triumphal hymn of joy, adapted from Psalm 98 by Isaac Watts. Even though the angels are not mentioned, one can almost hear them making their pronouncement of royal birth as the words to this seasonal hymn are sung with exuberance. Not only are the angels not mentioned in this Christmas song, but neither are the shepherds or the wise men. The song focuses solely on the baby whose birth is being announced, declaring the arrival of the long-awaited Messiah. There is an air of excitement that permeates this hymn.

"Joy to the World!" is taken from Psalm 98:4–6, which says, "Shout joyfully to the Lord, all the earth; Break forth in song, rejoice, and sing praises. . . . Shout joyfully before the Lord, the King." Originally, this psalm was written as a song of rejoicing for (Jehovah) God's protection of the Jewish people, and in anticipation of the day when God would set up His earthly kingdom. Isaac Watts, however, took the words from this psalm and turned them into an expression of praise to the newborn King. When this song first appeared in Watts' hymnal of 1719, it was titled "The Messiah's Coming and Kingdom." Lowell Mason, an American church musician, is thought to have adapted its music from some of the phrases from George Frideric Handel's *Messiah,* which was first performed in 1742. From the combined talents of an English literary genius of the eighteenth century, the German-born musical giant, and a nineteenth-century American choir director and educator, this great hymn came into its present state.

Just As I Am

Words by Charlotte Elliott (1789–1871)
Music by William B. Bradbury (1816–1868)

1. Just as I am, with-out one plea, But that Thy blood was shed for me, And that Thou bidst me come to Thee, O

Lamb of God,——— I come! I come!——— A - men.

2. *Just as I am, and waiting not*
   To rid my soul of one dark blot,
   To Thee whose blood can cleanse
      each spot,
   O Lamb of God, I come! I come!

3. *Just as I am, though tossed about*
   With many a conflict, many a doubt,
   Fightings and fears within, without,
   O Lamb of God, I come! I come!

4. *Just as I am, poor, wretched, blind;*
   Sight, riches, healing of the mind,
   Yea, all I need in Thee to find,
   O Lamb of God, I come! I come!

5. *Just as I am, Thou wilt receive,*
   Wilt welcome, pardon, cleanse,
      relieve,
   Because Thy promise I believe,
   O Lamb of God, I come! I come!

*T*his soul-winning song was written by Charlotte Elliott, born in 1789, a woman who was stricken by a serious illness when she was just thirty-two years old. As a result, Charlotte was confined to bed for the next half-century. Charlotte's father, the Reverend Henry Venn Elliott, was an Evangelical minister who lived in the resort community of Brighton, England, an area considered to be a religious stronghold in Victorian times. During her fifty years as an invalid, Charlotte wrote hundreds of hymns, many of which were published in hymn collections such as *The Invalids Hymn Book* and *Hours of Sorrow Cheered and Comforted.*

Written in 1834, "Just As I Am" came into being during a time when Harry Elliott, Charlotte's brother, was raising funds to build a college in Brighton. His original purpose for the college was to educate the daughters of four clergymen. The entire Elliott family was involved in helping put together a bazaar to raise money for the school. Charlotte, because of her illness, felt useless because she could not help. And yet, as she sat there all alone, she began to sense a contentment come over her. As she did, she composed the verses to this lovely hymn, which has brought comfort and strength to countless souls through the years. Her inspiration for the verses came from the words that had been spoken to her twelve years earlier by a Swiss evangelist, Dr. Cesar Malan. When she had tried to explain to Dr. Malan her unworthiness to come to Christ, his response was to come "just as you are."

"Just As I Am" first appeared in leaflet form in 1835, and all the proceeds from its sale went to St. Mary's Hall, the school Charlotte's brother was busy raising money to build. The sales from Charlotte's hymn brought in more money for the school than did the entire bazaar itself. This song is probably most famous today as the hymn that is sung during the altar calls at the Billy Graham Crusades.

For the early African-American believers, this song brought much healing. Rejected and outcast as they were, "Just As I Am" was an invitation from God to come to Him, and a promise that they would be accepted, regardless of their lot in life.

Leaning on the Everlasting Arms

Words by Elisha A. Hoffman (1839–1929)
Music by Anthony J. Showalter (1858–1924)

what a peace is mine, Lean-ing on the ev - er - last-ing arms.

Chorus

Lean - ing, lean - ing, Safe and se-cure from

(Lean-ing on Je-sus, lean-ing on Je-sus)

all a - larms; Lean - ing, lean - ing,

(Lean-ing on Je - sus, lean - ing on Je - sus)

Lean - ing on the ev - er - last - ing arms.

2. *O how sweet to walk in this
     pilgrim way,
   Leaning on the everlasting arms;
   O how bright the path grows from
     day to day,
   Leaning on the everlasting arms.*

3. *What have I to dread, what have I
     to fear,
   Leaning on the everlasting arms?
   I have blessed peace with my Lord
     so near,
   Leaning on the everlasting arms.*

*E*lisha A. Hoffman, the author of this hymn and a licensed preacher in the Evangelical United Brethren Church, served in the ministry for almost ninety years. He wrote numerous songs, many of which were included in Sunday school songbooks such as *Happy Songs for Sunday School, 1876* and *Sunday School Songs, 1880.* Some of his better-known songs are "Is Your All on the Altar?," "Are You Washed in the Blood?," and "I Must Tell Jesus."

Anthony J. Showalter, who wrote the music to this hymn, was a Presbyterian layman who conducted singing classes and Bible study groups and revival services in South Carolina, Georgia, and Alabama. One day in 1888 he received two letters, each from friends he had met while holding services in South Carolina. Both of these friends had written to Showalter expressing their grief at having just lost their wives. The women had died within a day or two of each other.

Showalter, in seeking some way to comfort his bereaved friends, wrote them letters quoting Deuteronomy 33:27, which says, "The eternal God is your refuge, And underneath are the everlasting arms." Even as he wrote the words to the verse, he tried to remember a hymn based on them, but he could not think of one. It was then that he decided to write one himself.

Sitting down at the piano, Showalter wrote the music and the words of the chorus, but was unable to come up with suitable verses. He sent what he had written to another minister from Pennsylvania, the Reverend Elisha A. Hoffman, author of the well-known hymn "I Must Tell Jesus," as well as "Glory to His Name," which is also known as "Down at the Cross." Hoffman liked the music and the chorus, and was able to compose verses to fit Showalter's music and theme. He sent the hymn back to Showalter, who then introduced the hymn at the Pine Log Methodist Church in Pine Log, Georgia, by singing it to the congregation. "Leaning on the Everlasting Arms" was first published in 1887 in the *Glad Evangel for Revival, Camp and Evangelistic Meetings Hymnal.*

A common saying in the African-American church, even today, comes from this song. When someone asks, "Sister So-and-So, how are you doing today?" the answer is often, "Oh, I'm leaning on the Lord!"

Lift Him Up
(How to Reach the Masses)

Words by Johnson Oatman Jr.
Music by B. B. Beall

1. How to reach the mass-es, men of ev-'ry birth, For an
an-swer Je-sus gave the key: "And__ I, if I be lift-ed
up from the earth, Will draw all men un-to Me."

Chorus

Lift Him up,——— Lift Him up,——— Still He
(Lift the pre-cious Sav-ior up, Lift the pre-cious Sav-ior up)

speaks from e-ter-ni-ty: "And— I, if I be lift-ed

up from the earth, Will draw all men un-to Me."

2. Oh! the world is hungry for the
   Living Bread,
   Lift the Savior up for them to see;
   Trust Him, and do not doubt the
   words that He said,
   "I'll draw all men unto Me."

3. Don't exalt the preacher, don't
   exalt the pew,
   Preach the Gospel simple, full and
   free;

Prove Him and you will find that
   promise is true,
   "I'll draw all men unto Me."

4. Lift Him up by living as a
   Christian ought,
   Let the world in you the Savior see;
   Then men will gladly follow Him
   who once taught,
   "I'll draw all men unto Me."

*T*he author of this popular hymn, Reverend Johnson Oatman Jr., was an ordained minister who did not have his own congregation. Instead he chose to become involved in his father's business, and later managed an insurance agency. His focus was on the writing of sacred music, including "The Hallelujah Side," "Hand in Hand with Jesus," "Higher Ground," "Count Your Blessings," and "No, Not One."

"Lift Him Up" is typical of the hymns that have been "gospelized" in the African-American church. Often, to get our "spiritual blood" flowing in a service, the preacher announces this song, and I get excited just hearing the electric organ start up. The organist's feet start dancing on the pedals, hands start clapping, tambourines start shaking—and we come alive!

"Gospelizing" hymns was a common practice in the African-American church. While appreciating and desiring to preserve the beauty and majesty of the original message of the hymns, worshippers also wanted to adapt the words and music to fit their needs and circumstances. The black church has always been a "church of emotion." The religious practices of African-American worship, as well as the African-American culture itself, have been greatly influenced by their roots in African culture.

As early as the hush harbor meetings of plantation slaves, when black churches were first established, African-Americans did not entirely throw out the sophisticated hymns they had learned from white Christians. Instead, they adopted them as their own while adapting them to their culture and needs. These reworked hymns were influenced by African religious music, the African call-and-response song, European and American religious and secular songs, and various African-American language dialects. Although some melodies were kept intact when these hymns were gospelized, others were changed, through different rhythms and harmonies, to reflect the black worship experience. John Newton's "Amazing Grace" and Fanny Crosby's "Close to Thee" are just a couple of examples of these gospelized hymns.

A Mighty Fortress Is Our God

Words and Music by Martin Luther (1483–1546)

1. A might-y for - tress is__ our__ God, A bul-wark nev-er fail - ing; Our help-er He__ a - mid__ the__ flood of mor-tal ills pre - vail - ing: For still our an - cient__ foe Doth seek to work us

woe; His craft and power are— great, And armed with— cru-el

hate, On earth is not his e - qual. A - men.

2. Did we in our own strength confide,
   Our striving would be losing,
   Were not the right Man on our side,
   The Man of God's own choosing.
   Dost ask who that may be?
   Christ Jesus, it is He—
   Lord Sabaoth, His name,
   From age to age the same—
   And He must win the battle.

3. And though this world, with devils
      filled,
   Should threaten to undo us,
   We will not fear, for God hath
      willed
   His truth to triumph through us.
   The prince of darkness grim—

We tremble not for him;
His rage we can endure,
For lo! his doom is sure—
One little word shall fell him.

4. That word above all earthly
      pow'rs—
   No thanks to them, abideth;
   The Spirit and the gifts are ours
   Through Him who with us sideth.
   Let goods and kindred go,
   This mortal life also;
   The body they may kill:
   God's truth abideth still—
   His kingdom is forever.

*T*he Bible says that "God is our refuge and strength, always ready to help in times of trouble." How meaningful that verse of Scripture must have been to Martin Luther as he penned this famous hymn. Often called the father of Protestantism, Martin Luther was a Roman Catholic clergyman who was so powerfully affected by the grace of God—particularly as expressed in Romans 1:17, which declares that "the just shall live by faith," that he initiated what is known as the Reformation. Although many others were instrumental in the Reformation, Martin Luther is by far the name most commonly associated with its beginnings. The early followers of this movement were often called "Protest-ants" (due to Luther's protests against the church), or "Lutherans," like the denomination that is still in existence today.

"A Mighty Fortress Is Our God" was written during one of the most difficult times in Luther's struggle with the Roman Catholic Church. Somewhat like the early African-American believers, Luther was persecuted, an outcast to many. His strong stand against what he saw as the immoral and unbiblical practices of the Catholic Church (such as the "selling of indulgences," i.e., the purchasing of forgiveness) made him very unpopular with the church's hierarchy and even put his life in danger. When he was called to Rome to answer to charges of heresy and insubordination, Luther managed to escape to Wittenberg, but was excommunicated from the Church in 1520. Written in Coburg, Germany, "A Mighty Fortress Is Our God" was Luther's call to spiritual battle. The music, now world-famous, is thought to have been developed by Luther from an old Gregorian melody. The powerful and uplifting tone of this song has resulted in its adoption as a battle cry in many national crises. It has even been called the "Marseillaise" of the Reformation, having been sung by many whose faith was being put to the test. It was not unusual to hear it sung in the streets by martyrs being led to their deaths, or by people being sent into exile. The army of Gustavus Adolphus sang it in 1631 before the battle of Leipzig. Again, in 1632, it was the battle hymn of Adolphus and his army at Lutzen, where the king was killed but the army was victorious. Time and time again, when the men and events of the Reformation are commemorated, this hymn is sung with pride and heartfelt gratitude. At Luther's monument in Wittenberg, the city where Luther started the Reformation by nailing his Ninety-five Theses to the castle church's door, the first line of the hymn is engraved for all to see.

Near the Cross

Words by Fanny J. Crosby (1820–1915)
Music by William H. Doane (1832–1916)

1. Je - sus, keep me near the cross; There a pre-cious foun-tain,
Free to all, a heal-ing stream, Flows from Cal-vary's moun-tain.

Chorus

In the cross, in the cross, Be my glo-ry ev - er,
Till my rap-tured soul shall find Rest be-yond the riv-er.

2. Near the cross, a trembling soul,
   Love and mercy found me;
   There the Bright and Morning Star
   Sheds its beams around me.

3. Near the cross! O Lamb of God,
   Bring its scenes before me;
   Help me walk from day to day
   With its shadow o'er me.

4. *Near the cross I'll watch and wait,*   *Till I reach the golden strand*
   Hoping, trusting ever,   *Just beyond the river.*

*S*ince its publication in 1869, the simple yet profound words to Fanny Crosby's "Near the Cross" have spoken to many hearts and blessed many listeners. Fanny's blindness, though a handicap in many ways, served to keep her focused on her Savior—near the cross. And her handicap certainly did not hamper her creativity in any way. Fanny authored approximately 8,000 hymn texts in her lifetime, setting them to existing tunes. "Near the Cross" was set to music written by William Howard Doane, Fanny's principle collaborator. Doane, a wealthy and successful businessman in Cincinnati, was composer and publisher of numerous gospel songs. Much of the new music of the African-American composers was a type of hymn-like composition similar to those penned by white composers such as William B. Bradbury, Robert Lowry, and Doane. When Doane died he willed much of his fortune to be used in the construction of the Doane Memorial Music Building at Moody Bible Institute in Chicago, as well as to other charities.

"Near the Cross" is a call back to the basics of Christianity. One of the strengths of the African-American church is its foundation on the simplicity of the Gospel message. From its slave-days inception, black Christianity in America has revolved around a deep love and dedication to the Son of God, who loved them enough to die in their place. People in hardship—especially the slaves—relate easily and empathetically to someone being humbled and abused. Realizing that Jesus had taken that abuse for them willingly and without complaint drew enthusiastic and grateful response from these new converts. Songs like "Near the Cross" were instrumental in reminding African-American worshippers of the roots of their faith in general, and the roots of the black church in particular.

O For a Thousand Tongues

Words by Charles Wesley (1707–1788)
Music by Carl G. Glaser

1. O for a thou - sand tongues to sing

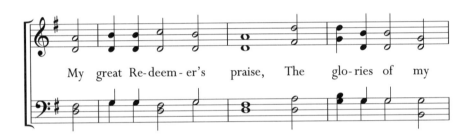

My great Re-deem-er's praise, The glo-ries of my

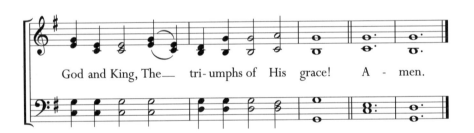

God and King, The— tri-umphs of His grace! A - men.

2. My gracious Master and my God,
   Assist me to proclaim,
   To spread through all the earth
   abroad
   The honors of Thy name.

3. Jesus! the name that charms our
   fears,
   That bids our sorrows cease,
   'Tis music in the sinner's ears,
   'Tis life and health and peace.

4. He breaks the pow'r of canceled sin,
   He sets the pris'ner free,
   His blood can make the foulest
      clean—
   His blood availed for me.

5. He speaks, and listening to His
      voice
   New life the dead receive;
   The mournful, broken hearts rejoice,
   The humble poor believe.

6. Hear Him, ye deaf; His praise, ye
   dumb,

Your loosened tongues employ;
Ye blind, behold your Savior come;
And leap, ye lame, for joy.

7. See all your sins on Jesus laid;
   The Lamb of God was slain,
   His soul was once an offering made
   For every soul of man.

8. Glory to God and praise and love
   Be ever, ever giv'n
   By saints below and saints above—
   The Church in earth and heav'n.

*O*ne of the most famous of Charles Wesley's hymns, "O For a Thousand Tongues" has the special honor of being placed as the first hymn in every edition of the Methodist hymnal. This song, originally with eighteen stanzas, was written by Wesley in May 1739 to commemorate the first year of his conversion to what he called "true religion." In 1740 the hymn was published in Wesley's *Hymns and Sacred Poems.*

It is believed that the very first verse of this majestic hymn was inspired by Peter Bohler, a Moravian preacher, who said, "Had I a thousand tongues, I would praise Him with them all." Several changes of phrases and words have often been made to this hymn; entire verses have even been omitted from present-day hymnals. Yet this beautiful hymn endures, cherished and favored throughout the church. It has been set to several different tunes, the most common being "Richmond," by Thomas Haweis (1734–1820). Methodists have used "Lydia," by Thomas Phillips (1735–1805); Anglicans favored the tune by Henry Harington, a tune referred to by several names, including "Landsdowne," "Harington," "Orlingburg," "Bath," and "Retirement." The vigorous "Lyngham," by Thomas Jarman (1782–1862) divides the second half of each verse between men and women in a very effective way.

I remember one Sunday afternoon in 1995 when I stopped to chat with "Mother" LaBeet after service. We greeted one another and began to talk about the goodness and mercy of God. "He's sure enough good and faithful," she said. "I've known Him for almost eighty years now, and I've known Him to be true. Oh, I don't have tongues enough to praise Him!"

O How I Love Jesus

Words by Frederick Whitfield (1829–1904)
American Melody

1. There is a name— I love to hear, I love to sing— its worth;— It sounds like mu - sic in my ear, The sweet - est name on earth.—

Chorus

O, how I love Je - sus, O, how I love Je - sus,——

O, how I love Je - sus, Be - cause he first loved me!——

2. It tells me of a Savior's love,
Who died to set me free;
It tells me of His precious blood,
The sinner's perfect plea.

3. It tells me what my Father hath
In store for ev'ry day,
And though I tread a darksome
  path,
Yields sunshine all the way.

4. It tells of One whose loving heart
Can feel my deepest woe,
Who in each sorrow bears a part,
That none can bear below.

*F*rederick Whitfield was the author of this popular hymn. He was an Anglican church clergyman who is credited with having written more than thirty books of religious verse. The actual origin of the tune is not known, but it is a typical, lilting nineteenth-century American folk song. This type of song was often used in the campground meetings that were so popular in that time, where people gathered together to worship in natural settings. As is true with many gospel-type hymns, the melody's power lies in the arrangement and choral harmonies.

The text of "O How I Love Jesus" originally consisted of eight stanzas. These verses, some of which are no longer contained in the present-day hymnals, are quite interesting in their context:

> *It tells me of a Father's smile*
> *That beams upon His child.*
> *It cheers me through this little while,*
> *Through deserts waste and wild.*

> *It bids my trembling soul rejoice,*
> *And dries each rising tear.*
> *It tells me in a still small voice,*
> *To trust and not to fear.*

First published in 1855, "O How I Love Jesus," with its simply stated, lifting musical testimony, has become another Sunday school favorite, having been translated into various languages and included in numerous hymnals over the years, including Whitfield's own collection, *Sacred Poems and Prose*. The words to this mighty hymn express so well the feelings of gratitude of so many believers as we reflect on all that Christ has done and continues to do for us every day.

Rock of Ages

Words by Augustus M. Toplady (1740–1778)
Music by Thomas Hastings (1784–1872)

1. Rock of a - ges, cleft for me, Let me

hide my-self in Thee; Let the wa - ter and the blood,

From Thy wound - ed side which flowed, Be of sin the dou - ble

cure, Save from wrath and make me pure. A - men.

2. Could my tears forever flow,
Could my zeal no languor know,
These for sin could not atone—
Thou must save, and Thou alone:
In my hand no price I bring,
Simply to Thy cross I cling.

3. Not the labors of my hands
Can fulfill Thy law's demands;
Could my zeal no respite know,
Could my tears for ever flow,
All for sin could not atone;
Thou must save, and Thou alone.

4. Nothing in my hand I bring,
Simply to the cross I cling;
Naked, come to Thee for dress;
Helpless, look to Thee for grace;
Foul, I to the fountain fly;
Wash me, Saviour, or I die.

5. While I draw this fleeting breath,
When my eyes shall close in death,
When I rise to worlds unknown,
And behold Thee on Thy throne,
Rock of ages, cleft for me,
Let me hide myself in Thee.

*R*ock of Ages" author Augustus Montague Toplady was born in Farn-ham, Surrey, England, the son of an army officer. He was educated at Westminster School and Trinity College in Dublin. At the age of sixteen he was converted to Evangelical Christianity when he heard a sermon preached in an Irish barn. He was later ordained into the Church of En-gland and became curate of Blagdon in Somerset in 1762. In 1774, suffer-ing from consumption and obsessed with the subject of sin, Toplady moved to London. It was there that he composed 133 hymns, including "Rock of Ages," which appeared in an article he wrote for the *Gospel Magazine* in March 1776. In it he described this hymn as "a living and dying prayer for the holiest believer in the world."

Dr. John Julian, author and compiler of the *Dictionary of Hymnody,* said there was no other hymn that could be compared to "Rock of Ages" in its grasp upon the English-speaking world. As popular today as in times past, "Rock of Ages" is a perennial favorite. The Victorians listed it as one of their most beloved hymns. It is reported that Prince Albert repeated its words over and over again as he lay dying at Windsor Castle. It was trans-lated into Greek, Latin, and Italian by English prime minister William E. Gladstone. In fact, it was sung at Gladstone's funeral, which caused the writer A. C. Benson to comment, "To have written words which should come home to people in moments of high, deep and passionate emotion; consecrating, consoling, uplifting . . . there can hardly be anything better worth doing than that."

Performed by countless singers through the years, "Rock of Ages" was one of gospel great Mahalia Jackson's favorites—and she sang it gloriously! Sitting in my den in Tougaloo, Mississippi, where I was a professor at Tougaloo College, I listened to Jackson's rendition of this hymn at least a hundred times over one particular weekend. It was a time in my life when I felt devastated, despairing, fearful, hopeless. Mahalia's voice, reaching out from the depths of her soul, touched my life that weekend in a powerful way. Her voice was as much a gift from God as was the hymn itself. What comfort and encouragement I found as I listened to the eternal truth pro-claimed in this song!

The Solid Rock

Words by Edward Mote (1797–1874)
Music by William B. Bradbury (1816–1868)

1. My hope is built on noth-ing less Than Je-sus' blood and righ-teous-ness; I dare not trust the sweet-est frame, But whol-ly lean on Je-sus' name.

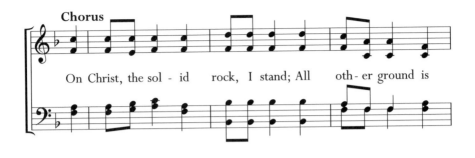

On Christ, the sol - id   rock, I stand; All   oth - er ground is

sink - ing sand, All   oth - er ground is   sink - ing sand.

2. When darkness veils His lovely face,
   I rest on His unchanging grace;
   In ev'ry high and stormy gale
   My anchor holds within the veil.

3. His oath, His covenant, His blood
   Support me in the whelming flood;

When all around my soul gives way,
He then is all my hope and stay.

4. When He shall come with trumpet
      sound,
   O may I then in Him be found,
   Dressed in His righteousness alone,
   Faultless to stand before the throne.

*B*orn in 1797, "The Solid Rock" author Edward Mote grew up in England with absolutely no training about God or the Bible. And yet, at the age of sixteen, he was converted to Christ, later settling in a suburb of London where he became a successful cabinetmaker and was known in the community as a devoted church layman. In talking of his youth, prior to his conversion, Mote said, "My Sundays were spent on the streets [of London] in play. . . . So ignorant was I that I did not know there was a God."

One day after his conversion, as Mote was walking to work, the thought occurred to him that he should write a hymn. By the time he reached his shop he had decided on the chorus: "On Christ, the solid Rock, I stand; All other ground is sinking sand." He continued to think about the hymn as he worked, and by the end of the day he had added four stanzas.

Then, on the following Sunday, Mote went to visit a preacher friend whose wife was gravely ill. As he sat and read from the Bible and prayed with her, he looked around for a hymnal to sing from, but couldn't find one. Instead, he reached into his pocket and pulled out the paper on which he had written "The Solid Rock," and sang it to her. Mote was so pleased that his composition had brought this dying woman comfort that he made up a thousand copies and distributed them among his friends and acquaintances.

Mote eventually became a Baptist preacher, and during the course of his lifetime he penned 150 hymn texts. Just before he died, he said, "I think I am going to heaven, yes, I am nearing port. The truths I have preached I am now living upon, and they will do to die upon. Ah! The precious blood which takes away all our sins. It is this which makes peace with God."

Along with the music to this hymn, William B. Bradbury wrote the tunes for "Jesus Loves Me" and "Just As I Am," both in this book, and "He Leadeth Me," "Depth of Mercy," "Even Me," and "Sweet Hour of Prayer."

Take the Name of Jesus

Words by Lydia Baxter (1809–1874)
Music by William H. Doane (1832–1916)

1. Take the name of Je - sus with you,

sweet!____ Hope of earth and joy of heav'n.

sweet, how sweet!)

2. *Take the name of Jesus ever,*
   As a shield from ev'ry snare;
   If temptations round you gather,
   Breathe that holy name in prayer.

3. *O the precious name of Jesus!*
   How it thrills our souls with joy,

When His loving arms receive us,
And His songs our tongues employ!

4. *At the name of Jesus bowing,*
   Falling prostrate at His feet,
   King of kings in heav'n we'll
       crown Him,
   When our journey is complete.

*L*ydia Baxter, the author of this lovely hymn, spent the majority of her life as a bedridden invalid. And yet her attitude remained cheerful and patient. The reason, she said, was because "I have a very special armor. I have the name of Jesus. When the tempter [devil] tries to make me blue or despondent, I mention the name of Jesus, and he can't get through to me anymore." All through Lydia's life she was known to those closest to her as an avid Bible student. She loved to talk about scriptural names and their meanings, such as Samuel, which means "asked of God"; Hannah, which means "grace"; and Sarah, which means "princess." Her favorite name, as she would tell anyone who would listen, was the name of Jesus.

"Take the Name of Jesus" was written when Lydia was sixty-five, just four years before her death in 1874. This hymn was often sung in the late nineteenth century during the Moody-Sankey evangelistic campaigns, which helped it to become a favorite of many. One of those who considered this hymn a favorite was my father, whom I affectionately refer to as Yancey Lee. He loved to listen to this song; he loved even more to sing it.

My father was born in 1898 in Thebes, Georgia. Growing up in a household with a mother and father in the ministry and his two older brothers pursuing theological studies in preparation for the ministry, he decided he didn't want any part of it. In fact, he ran from his calling into the ministry for many years, pursuing a law degree at Howard University in Washington, D.C., and Temple University in Philadelphia, Pennsylvania. He worked and saved his money for tuition, declaring he was not going to become a "poor old preacher."

Yancey Lee worked as a social worker at the University of Pennsylvania Hospital and stashed away a sizable amount of money for his educational expenses. However, in the 1920s banks were not yet federally secured. When the Great Depression hit in 1929, he lost all of his savings. It was at that point that he took stock of his life and realized he had been disobedient to God in running from the call to ministry. And so he set his heart to obey the Lord and entered the ministry of the A.M.E. church, becoming a true blessing to the churches he pastored for close to thirty years.

I can remember hearing my dad, in the midst of his preaching, break forth in his brilliant baritone voice to sing songs of praise to God. "Take the Name of Jesus" was just one of the songs that the former would-be lawyer sang from the bottom of his heart.

There Is a Fountain

Words by William Cowper (1731–1800)
American Melody

1. There— is a foun - tain filled with blood Drawn—

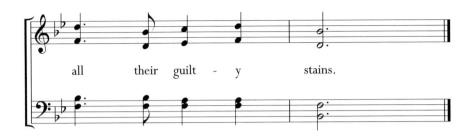

all   their   guilt - y   stains.

2. *The dying thief rejoiced to see*
   That fountain in his day,
   And there may I, though vile as he,
   Wash all my sins away;
   Wash all my sins away,
   Wash all my sins away;
   And there may I, though vile as he,
   Wash all my sins away.

3. *Dear dying Lamb, Thy precious*
       blood
   Shall never lose its pow'r,
   Till all the ransomed Church of God
   Be saved to sin no more;
   Be saved to sin no more,
   Be saved to sin no more;
   Till all the ransomed Church of God
   Be saved to sin no more.

4. *E'er since by faith I saw the stream*
   Thy flowing wounds supply,
   Redeeming love has been my theme
   And shall be till I die;
   And shall be till I die,
   And shall be till I die;
   Redeeming love has been my theme
   And shall be till I die.

5. *When this poor lisping, stamm'ring*
       tongue
   Lies silent in the grave,
   Then in a nobler, sweeter song,
   I'll sing Thy pow'r to save;
   I'll sing Thy pow'r to save,
   I'll sing Thy pow'r to save;
   Then in a nobler, sweeter song,
   I'll sing Thy pow'r to save.

*V*iewed by some as one of the finest of all English writers, William Cowper, author of "There Is a Fountain," suffered from an emotional life that was full of great trial and turmoil. Cowper's father wanted his son to study law, and wanting to please his father, Cowper reluctantly obeyed. But by the time he had completed his studies, the idea of appearing before the bar for his final examination frightened him so badly that he had a mental breakdown and even attempted suicide. As a result, he spent eighteen months in an insane asylum. During that long, dark time, however, something happened that changed Cowper's life. Through the daily reading of the Scriptures, he came to a personal relationship with Jesus Christ. He was thirty-three years old.

Three years after his conversion, Cowper moved to Olney, England, where John Newton pastored the parish Anglican church. They met, and for nearly twenty years Cowper and Newton worked and worshipped together. Soon they had become close friends and began to collaborate on the famous *Olney Hymns*. This hymnal, containing 349 hymns, is considered by many to be one of the most important contributions ever made to the field of evangelical hymnody. Sixty-seven of those hymns were written by Cowper; the remainder were penned by Newton.

Originally titled "Peace for the Fountain Opened," this particular hymn is vivid in its imagery, and is based on Zechariah 13:1, which says: "On that day a fountain will be opened to the house of David and the inhabitants of Jerusalem, to cleanse them from sin and impurity."

We're Marching to Zion

Words by Isaac Watts (1674–1748)
Music by Robert Lowry (1826–1899)

in a song with sweet ac-cord, And thus sur -
(And thus sur-round the

round the throne, And thus sur-round the throne.___
throne, And thus sur - round the throne)___

Chorus

We're march - ing to Zi - on, Beau-ti-ful, beau-ti-ful
(We're march-ing on to Zi - on)

Zi - on; We're march-ing up-ward to Zi - on,___ The
(Zi - on, Zi-on)

beau - ti - ful cit - y of God.___

2. *Let those refuse to sing*
   Who never knew our God;
   But children of the heav'nly King,
   But children of the heav'nly King,
   May speak their joys abroad,
   May speak their joys abroad.

3. *This hill of Zion yields*
   A thousand sacred sweets
   Before we reach the heav'nly fields,

   Before we reach the heav'nly fields,
   Or walk the golden streets,
   Or walk the golden streets.

4. *Then let our songs abound,*
   And ev'ry tear be dry;
   We're marching through
      Immanuel's ground,
   We're marching through
      Immanuel's ground,
   To fairer worlds on high,
   To fairer worlds on high.

*I*saac Watts, the author of many other popular hymns besides "We're Marching to Zion," once found himself in the middle of a major controversy. And he wasn't the only one. Two long-standing questions in the church have been: (1) Which should we sing in our church services, psalms or hymns? and (2) Should we adopt contemporary gospel sounds or stick with the traditional music? Sadly, these questions have been allowed to develop into heated controversy in some churches, even causing splits among congregations.

Watts, a longtime champion of what is sometimes called the "humanly composed" hymn, was opposed to those who insisted on singing only the traditional psalms. Fortunately, even as tempers flared, many churches were able to come to a compromise. Traditional psalms would be sung in the early part of the church service, with a closing hymn sung at the end. However, during the closing hymn, some parishioners chose not to sing; others simply left the service early.

"We're Marching to Zion" may very well have been written by Watts in part as a response to criticisms of what many called "Watts's Whims." A couple of pointed lines in the song seem to speak directly to those critics: "Let those refuse to sing Who never knew our God; But children of the heav'nly King . . . May speak their joys abroad."

Some controversy still exists today as to what types of songs are appropriate for worship. Although it is understandable that we each have different preferences, those preferences should not bring division within the church. In the words of Augustine, "Let there be in the essentials, unity. In all non-essentials, liberty. In all things, charity."

Watts has always been a favorite in the African-American church. Although Wesley's and Newton's hymns are also popular, it is Isaac Watts's lyrics that speak most deeply to the African-American congregation. Even today, in some communities that still practice the lining-out tradition, all lining hymns are referred to as "Dr. Watts."

What a Friend We Have in Jesus

Words by Joseph Scriven (1820–1886)
Music by Charles C. Converse (1832–1918)

1. What a Friend we have in Je-sus,   All our sins and griefs to bear!

What a priv-i-lege to car-ry   Ev-'ry-thing to God in   prayer!

O what peace we oft-en for-feit,   O what need-less pain we bear,

All be-cause we do not car - ry   Ev- 'ry-thing to God in   prayer!

2. *Have we trials and temptations?*
   Is there trouble anywhere?
   We should never be discouraged—
   Take it to the Lord in prayer.
   Can we find a friend so faithful
   Who will all our sorrows share?
   Jesus knows our ev'ry weakness—
   Take it to the Lord in prayer.

3. *Are we weak and heavy-laden,*
   Cumbered with a load of care?
   Precious Savior, still our refuge—
   Take it to the Lord in prayer.
   Do thy friends despise, forsake thee?
   Take it to the Lord in prayer;
   In His arms He'll take and shield
   *   thee—*
   Thou wilt find a solace there.

To look at this author's beginnings, one would expect him to have lived a life of ease and pleasure. Born in Ireland to a wealthy, devoted family, Joseph Scriven was able to afford the best of everything, including an education. However, his dreams of a military career were dashed by chronic poor health. Then, on the night before his wedding, tragedy struck. His bride-to-be was drowned, and his heart was broken.

Leaving Ireland at the age of twenty-five, he emigrated to Canada, settling first at Rice Lake and then at Port Hope, Ontario. There he made a living as a tutor, devoting his free time to working without pay among the poor and destitute, often giving away his clothes and other possessions. At last it seemed happiness was within his grasp when, once again, he became engaged. But once again his dreams were crushed as he watched his fiancée die after a brief illness. In October 1886 he drowned, and his body was found in a water-run near Rice Lake.

Before he died, however, he wrote a poem to his mother back in Ireland, wanting to comfort her in her illness. That poem became the much-beloved hymn "What a Friend We Have in Jesus," and was set to a tune by

Charles Converse. There is still some question as to whether Converse wrote the tune to fit Scriven's words or whether it was originally written for another song, then adapted to Scriven's words by Ira Sankey for the first edition of his *Gospel Hymns.*

When asked by a friend where he had gotten the words to "What a Friend We Have in Jesus," Joseph Scriven replied, "The Lord and I did it between us." I can certainly believe that. This precious hymn has such special meaning for me, primarily because it was my mother's favorite. She was always humming it! To this day I can't hear this song without thinking of her. It seems appropriate, somehow, knowing Scriven wrote it for his own mother.

IV.

contemporary gospel songs

Songs of Crouch, Hawkins, Smallwood, Franklin, and others
1960–Present

I sing because I'm happy! I sing because I'm free!
His eye is on the sparrow! That's the reason why I sing.

Glory, hallelujah! You're the reason why I sing.

*E*ven as the heyday of depression-era gospel music was coming to a close, the freedom struggle in the South was beginning in earnest. The spirituals that had been born in slavery were rediscovered, as demonstrators—both black and white—transformed these historic songs into "freedom songs," taking the original words and adapting them to fit the immediate social context of the times. It wasn't that these songs were new; they were simply updated, gaining popularity among some who had never heard them before. The words of the freedom songs—and the message behind the words—bridged the generation gap, as old and young joined together in a struggle symbolized in music.

It is not surprising, then, that the transfer of gospel influence into the world of entertainment became more prominent than ever. As radio and television transmissions of freedom marches popularized this soul-stirring music, the concept of "soul" music was also coming into its own. In reference to soul music, gospel great Mahalia Jackson said, "After all, we invented it. All this mess you hear calling itself soul ain't nothing but warmed-over gospel." Many who made it as Top 40 stars, including Ray Charles, Bobby "Blue" Bland, Wilson Pickett, James Brown, Al Green, and Aretha Franklin, were either former gospel singers or were at least strongly influenced by the gospel music sound. Some, like Al Green, have even returned to singing gospel after having succeeded in the secular music world.

Whether they crossed over or refused to defect, these singers were making an impact on American culture. And then, in 1969, the biggest commercial breakthrough in gospel history exploded onto the charts when the Edwin Hawkins Singers released "O Happy Day," a reworking of a traditional Baptist hymn, which sold two million copies. Suddenly people who had never heard or sung gospel in their lives, and cared nothing for its roots, were humming and singing along with this best-seller and clamoring for more. It was this success that helped create what we now call modern or contemporary gospel, which is the type of gospel music we will be looking at in this final section.

As popular as this new gospel is, it is not without its critics. As in the days of Thomas A. Dorsey, there are those who see this pop-oriented approach to gospel as sacrilegious. In Dorsey's era, the traditionalists were concerned about the increasing secularization of what they felt should remain sacred. In fact, the controversy goes back even farther. Isaac Watts was criticized—even shunned by some—for his compositions, which many referred to as "Watts's Whims" rather than hymns. They were a departure from the norm, and therefore were eyed suspiciously. Today we look back on them as traditional and cherished hymns of the past.

Despite the critics who view contemporary gospel music as being too "worldly" or secular, I believe the day will come when, like "Watts's Whims" and Dorsey's "sacrilegious" gospel songs, modern gospel will be cherished and sacred. In addition to reflecting the spirit of praise and worship so prevalent throughout the church at this hour, modern gospel music fulfills the biblical mandate from the apostle Paul to sing to one another in "psalms, hymns, and spiritual songs." Much of the music of Fred Hammond, Andrae Crouch, and Richard Smallwood contained in this section is based on passages from the Bible, particularly the Psalms. Kirk Franklin's "Savior More Than Life" is based on a favorite hymn by Fanny Crosby, "Savior, More Than Life to Me." In fact, many of today's gospel artists, such as Kurt Carr and Donnie McClurkin, are bringing back the traditional Watts-style hymns in their music. On Donnie McClurkin's 1996 release, *Donnie McClurkin, Donnie McClurkin,* he sings a classical/contemporary arrangement of the favorite "Holy, Holy, Holy, Lord God Almighty" as well as Thomas Dorsey's great gospel song "Search Me, Lord." And Arthur Freeman's "To You, Jesus" was written spontaneously as he was moved by the Spirit of God—a modern-day spiritual song.

It is as if the music of the church is coming full circle, as new "psalms, hymns, and spiritual songs" are being sung alongside revived spirituals and historical gospel songs, sometimes replacing the liturgy of the church, sometimes accompanying it. As the popularity of contemporary music written by African-American composers spreads via CDs, music videos, TV, radio, and concert halls, we hear the terms "urban gospel" and "urban praise" being used to describe much of it. We even see a revival of "blackened" music, as in the times of the "blackened hymns." This "blackened" music consists of praise and worship songs and choruses given an African-American flavor; they have been made especially popular through the

Integrity's Hosanna! Music and Maranatha! Music song collections and are sung with great fervor in churches throughout the land. As spirituals, historical gospel songs, and blackened hymns are revived and "psalms, hymns, and spiritual songs" are being sung and appreciated in secular settings as well as in the church, contemporary gospel music is accomplishing much of its purpose by spreading its sacred influence.

But regardless of how future generations view the impact of today's creeping secularization of contemporary gospel music, trends seem to indicate that it is here to stay. As of October 1993, there were 20 million gospel records sold. According to a 1992 Gallup Poll, 40 million people have bought gospel music at some time in their lives, and 31 million people have attended a gospel concert somewhere other than in church. It is not surprising, then, that the money moguls of the entertainment industry are scrambling to hop aboard the gospel music bandwagon. Even as some other areas of the music industry seem to be stagnant, gospel music is booming. As a result, many secular companies are looking to the Christian entertainment world for new direction. Buyouts and takeovers are becoming commonplace. Gaylord Entertainment, a Nashville-based entertainment conglomerate, recently signed a purchase agreement with Word Records for $110 million. Platinum Entertainment, Inc., purchased Intersound, Inc., for approximately $24 million in cash and $5 debentures (corporate securities, bonds). Sparrow and Starsong have reached distribution accords with large secular companies. With these kinds of deals being struck on a regular basis, it is obvious that mainstream companies' interest in gospel music is more than a passing fad.

But is it a good one? And what does it mean for gospel music's future? Dr. Bobby Jones, a gospel television show producer, is not optimistic. "It has been revealed to the big dogs that there is money to be made in this industry," he says. "But at what price? We [gospel artists] can't treat the music as if it were a secular form just because the 'big boys' move in. We have to maintain the music's sacredness." Tony Heilbut, noted authority on gospel music and author of *The Gospel Sound,* agrees. "Instead of looking to the hill [a biblical reference meaning 'looking to God for help and success'], it looks to the charts."

On the other hand, many within the gospel music industry see this merging with the "big boys" in the secular marketplace as a new avenue of spreading the true meaning of gospel music to those who would not otherwise hear it. Tramaine Hawkins, one of the more popular contemporary gospel singers, says, "We're singing the words of life in accordance with what we believe in." Walter Stewart, a gospel-program host on both radio and television, is a traditionalist, but with a pragmatic bent. He believes that young people are "better trained musically and have a greater knowledge of instrumentation," and "If we don't use them [what some term 'worldly' instruments and styles—another criticism of the merging of secular and sacred] in the church, they're [the young people] going to go to the world." Chuck Myricks, vice president at Word Records, sees this merging of secular and sacred as an opportunity not only for "more money, television and hotel appearances," but also for "better distribution."

Another area of controversy that all this merging of secular and sacred raises is the fact that "black" gospel has, to a large degree, been taken over by whites. Grammy Award–winning artist Hezekiah Walker, though skeptical of the trend, says, "There are some Caucasian sisters and brothers who really love Black gospel and study it." Other die-hard gospel singers feel that it is the African-American history and experience that makes gospel music what it is. John P. Kee, a popular artist with fans on both the gospel and contemporary Christian charts, says, "Gospel music is a part of who I am as a person. It's the hand-clapping, foot-patting, throw-your-hands-up-in-the-air kind of music my granddaddy taught me as a child, and that can't be easily replicated."

The merging of sacred and secular—a marriage made in Heaven, or a sacrilegious sellout? With the distinctions between sacred and secular music receding markedly and the introduction into church services of instrumentation beyond the traditional piano and pipe organ, it is a question with no easy answer. But one thing is certain. The future of gospel music is bright, and its contemporary influence will be as powerful in America's culture as was its depression-era counterpart.

In fact, I believe it will be greater, simply because of the times we are living in. As difficult as the slave and depression eras were, these "last days" will be even more so for those who seek to stand by their beliefs without compromise. In our modern world, we like to think of tribulation and persecution as a thing of the past—but it is not so. Because we believe what the Bible teaches about these "end times," we in the church expect that things will get worse before they get better. But just as was the case in past times of tribulation, so it will be today. The fires of persecution will only drive us closer to the flame of God. As that flame burns brighter, the songs in our hearts will burst forth with more passion and commitment than ever before. And the message of hope upon which our songs are based will draw those who are searching for just such a hope. That is why we sing—and that is why, regardless of criticism or controversy over contemporary gospel trends, I rejoice in the future of this powerful music. Like the enslaved believers of the past, we too can "sing the songs of Zion in a strange land" because we know that "the Lord is [our] strength and song. And He has become [our] salvation." If the Lord is our strength and our song, how can we help but sing?

Bless His Holy Name

Psalm 103:1

Music by Andrae Crouch (born 1950)

*B*orn in Los Angeles, California, in 1950, Andrae Crouch, the author of this song, grew up singing in his father's Holiness church and began playing for church services when he was eleven years old. As a child he became a part of the Crouch Trio (composed of his brother, sister, and himself) and began performing on his father's Sunday-night radio broadcasts and preaching engagements. During his school years he performed with a group called COGIS; then, in 1968, he organized the Disciples, becoming their lead singer and pianist. His twin sister, Sandra, was also a part of the group.

Before long the Disciples were touring throughout the United States and abroad, and Andrae had become one of the leading gospel singers of the 1960s and '70s. His many accomplishments include the authoring of such songs as "I Don't Know Why Jesus Loved Me," "Through It All," and "The Blood Will Never Lose Its Power," the last two being included in this section. His albums *Live in London* and *Take Me Back* were so successful that other entertainers, including Elvis Presley and Pat Boone, recorded some of his songs. He has since received numerous awards from the music, recording, and entertainment industries, including an Academy Award nomination for best original score for the movie *The Color Purple*. He was the vocal arranger for Michael Jackson's "Man in the Mirror" and Madonna's "Like a Prayer." Having performed everywhere from small country churches to Carnegie Hall, Andrae has touched countless lives with his soul-stirring gospel renditions, which are as much preaching and teaching as they are singing. And as Andrae sings, audiences join in. They sing with him, they clap with him, their feet move to the beat—faster as he goes—and they are lifted to new heights with him as he worships his God.

Sung more often than just about any other contemporary chorus in modern Christendom, "Bless His Holy Name" is taken almost verbatim from Psalm 103. The Hebrew word for "bless," *barak,* means to gratefully praise God. The psalmist is instructing his soul "and all that is within" him to gratefully praise God for all the great things He has done. Andrae's song "Bless His Holy Name" certainly fulfills that directive.

The Blood Will Never Lose Its Power

Words and Music by Andrae Crouch (born 1950)

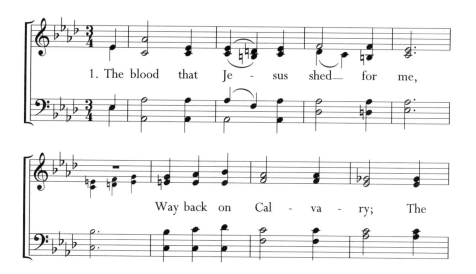

1. The blood that Je - sus shed— for me,

Way back on Cal - va - ry; The

blood that gives me strength from day to day,—— It will nev - er lose its power.——

2. *It soothes my doubts and calms my*
   fears,
   And it dries all my tears;

The blood that gives me strength
from day to day,
It will never lose its power.

*A*s in the days of the spirituals, the theme of the blood of Jesus is still a popular one in contemporary gospel music. The amazing thing about this particular song is that it was one of Andrae Crouch's first compositions—written when he was thirteen!

Andrae's career as a singer, songwriter, and performer began extremely early. His father, Bishop Benjamin J. Crouch, was the founder of the Christ Memorial Church of God in Christ in the San Fernando Valley of California, so it was not unusual that music—particularly spiritual and gospel music—would be a part of Andrae's life from an early age. Along with his twin sister Sandra, Andrae began singing when he was five years old. By the time he was ten, he and Sandra were singing in prisons.

Of course, Andrae's performances weren't always as well attended as they are today. At one of his very first concerts, only 200 of the 5,000 available seats were sold. Judy Spencer, executive vice president of

Andrae's first music publisher, Manna Records in Nashville, said, "In those days we weren't worried about getting his songs known around the world—we were worried about getting his songs known around town." Their attempts more than succeeded.

Before long, Andrae had made his mark across the United States. He is a three-time Dove Award winner whose music has broken down racial barriers. Back when his career was first getting off the ground, this sort of accomplishment was not taken for granted. In one instance, when he was about to perform at the national Quartet Convention in Nashville, the convention organizers nervously went on stage ahead of him. They wanted to diffuse any potential problems by explaining to the all-white audience of 3,000 that Andrae was black. They needn't have worried. Not only was Andrae Crouch warmly received, but his performance brought down the house.

Breathe into Me, Oh Lord

Psalm 119:25

Words and Music by Fred Hammond and David Ivey

1. When the bat - tle makes— me wea - ry, it seems that I've— lost ground,— It's so hard to hear— Your voice, — Lord,— with dis-trac-tion all— a - round,— I try to

lift___ my hands___ to give You praise,___

___ But then a spir-it of hea - vi-ness

tries to shield___ Your face. So I'm say-ing, Breathe,

Chorus

Breathe in-to me, oh Lord,___ The breath of___ life,___ So that my spir-

___ it would be whole,___ and my soul made___ right.___

Breathe in-to me, oh Lord,___ day by day,___ So that my heart

___ is pure___ be-fore___ You,___ al - ways,___ al -

ways.___ Un - to Thee, oh___ Lord,___ I will

lift up my soul,___ It's on-ly by Your hand___

that I can be made whole.____ So,

Lord, breathe on me   and   re-vive my spir-it with-in,

And I'll ne-ver   be   the   same.____

Chorus

Breathe in-to me, oh Lord,____   The breath of____ life,____

____ So that my spir - it would_ be whole,____   and my

soul made_ right.____   Breathe in-to me, oh Lord,____

day by____ day,____   So that my heart____ is pure   be-fore_

____ You,____   al - ways,____   al - ways.____ Con-dem-

na - tion tries— to hold me,   like a pris-on-er— in chains,—

—   And the weight— of— my bur-dens—   is

call - ing out— my   name.—   That's when I   lift up my

voice   to wor - ship   You, be-cause I know—   You prom-

ised You— would wash me,   Je - sus, wash me white— as

Bridge

snow.   Un - to Thee,   oh— Lord,—   I will

lift   up   my   soul,—   It's on-ly   by   Your hand—

—   that I   can   be   made   whole.—   So,

Lord,   let Your breath re-vive me a - gain,_____ And I'll

ne - ver   be   the   same,_____ And I'll

ne - ver   be   the   same,_____ And I'll

ne - ver   be   the   same._____

Chorus

Breathe in - to me, oh Lord,____   the breath of__ life,__

____ So that my spir - it would be whole,____ And my

soul made__ right.__   Breathe in- to me, oh Lord, __

day by __ day,__   So that my heart__ is pure__ be-fore__

__ You,-   al - ways,-   al - ways.__

*A*nother song taken from a psalm, "Breathe into Me, Oh Lord" is one of several on Fred Hammond's recording *The Spirit of David* (referring to King David, the most prolific of the biblical psalmists), released in 1996 with the Radical for Christ Singers. Like King David, Fred Hammond presents here Old Testament and New Testament scriptural songs, mostly from the Book of Psalms, and songs of praise. Here, in spite of much criticism of contemporary gospel because of its secularization, we see what has become a typical trend of this contemporary music toward psalms, hymns, and spiritual songs of old.

On this particular album, Hammond, often paraphrasing the Scriptures, composes songs in hymn style, such as this song. In another song on the album, Hammond takes his chorus directly from the Scriptures: "Oh give thanks unto the Lord, His mercy endureth forever." Psalm 47 is the basis for his song "Shout unto God," and "The Lord Is Good" is taken from Psalm 100:5. There are also modern-day hymns, such as "Success Is in Your Hand," based on the context of Psalm 37; and "Call Me Righteous," based on the text of Romans 4:5–8. A most magnificent song of worship and adoration is his "Blessing and Honor," based on Psalm 45, a glorious yet simple presentation of exaltation and glory to God.

On his album, *The Spirit of David,* Hammond includes a very well-known contemporary praise chorus, "When the Spirit of the Lord" (author unknown), based on 2 Samuel 6:14. Using an Israeli-style tune, Hammond takes it and sets it upon a typical contemporary arrangement of African-American rhythm and harmony, resulting in a modern-day gospel hymn that has become a favorite for many.

The Center of My Joy

Words by Gloria Gaither
Music by William J. Gaither and Richard Smallwood

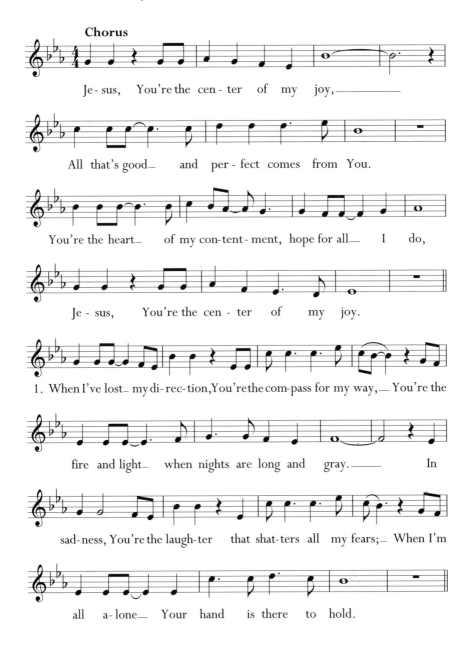

Chorus

Je- sus, You're the cen - ter of my joy,——

All that's good— and per - fect comes from You.

You're the heart— of my con-tent-ment, hope for all— I do,

Je - sus, You're the cen - ter of my joy.

1. When I've lost— my di- rec-tion, You're the com-pass for my way,— You're the

fire and light— when nights are long and gray.—— In

sad-ness, You're the laugh-ter that shat-ters all my fears;— When I'm

all a-lone— Your hand is there to hold.

2. You are why— I find plea-sure in the sim-ple things in life.— You're the

mu-sic in the mead-ows and the streams.——— The

voi-ces of the chil-dren, my fam-'ly and my home.— You're the

source and fin-ish of my high - est dreams.

Je - sus, You're the cen-ter of my joy,———

All that's good— and per - fect comes from You.

You're the heart— of my con-tent - ment, hope for all— I do,

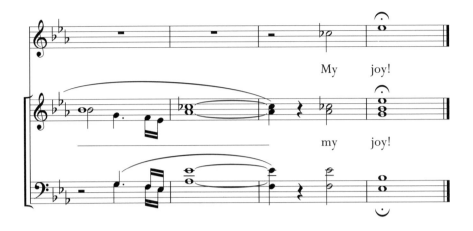

A ballad of praise and adoration, "The Center of My Joy," written by Richard Smallwood and Bill and Gloria Gaither, is typical of the type of "love song" or ballad that became popular throughout much of the church during the late 1960s and the '70s. Richard Smallwood has long been recognized as a pioneer in contemporary gospel music. He was part of the first college-based gospel choir, which was started at Howard University in 1965, in Washington, D.C. Smallwood, along with two other brilliant musicians, Henry Davis and Wesley Boyd, were African-American music majors at the prominent and predominantly black school. However, these talented students were not allowed to play their gospel music in the university's practice rooms. But it was not long before black students insisted on some major changes in the overall curriculum of the university. Such changes included the acknowledgment of black contributions to American culture, as well as the treatment of African-based history and traditions. Obviously, these changes included gospel music and the music students were allowed to practice such music in the practice studios. In addition, the study and performance of gospel music was incorporated into the music program. Smallwood and his group, the Richard Smallwood Singers, eventually became known for a choral effect that sounded like the old-fashioned Pentecostal shout.

Bill Gaither, a white singer and songwriter, is best known for his many gospel compositions as well as for his involvement in the Bill Gaither Trio, an extremely popular contemporary gospel group. With his wife, Gloria, another member of the trio, Gaither has written more than five hundred published songs, many of which are known and loved throughout the church. Smallwood and the Gaithers are a perfect example of the cross-racial appeal of contemporary gospel music, not only to listeners but also to writers and singers.

Church Medley

Traditional choruses
Arranged by Donnie McClurkin

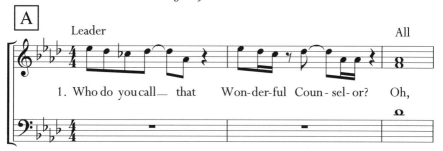

Ris-ing He jus - ti-fied,— freed me— for-ev - er!

One day— He's com-ing back, glo - ri - ous day!—

D

1. Send Him on down...(x2)

2

Lord, let Your Ho - ly Ghost

come on down!—

2

Send Him on down...(x2)

Lord, let Your Ho - ly Ghost come on down!—

A 2. He's a well of water, way down
   in my soul . . .

 3. I call Jesus that Wonderful
    Counselor! . . .

B 2. Who saved your soul? Jesus!
    Nobody else but Jesus!

 3. Who baptized you? Jesus!
    Nobody else but Jesus!

 4. I love to call Him Jesus!
    Nobody else but Jesus!
    Jesus, Jesus, Jesus, Jesus!

D 2. We can't do nothin' 'til You
    send Him on down.
    Lord, let Your Holy Ghost come
    on down!

E 2. Power to walk right . . .

 3. Power to talk right . . .

 4. Power to pray right . . .

 5. Power to sing right . . .

*T*he talented contemporary songwriter, arranger, choir director, and musician Donnie McClurkin arranged these individual choruses of various origins into a medley of praise. And what a medley this is! The first verses are from a traditional call-and-response-type spiritual, where the leader or soloist would lead out a line and the congregation or choir would respond with fragments of melody and text. Because the songs were commonly conceived spontaneously by individuals who did not read or write, call and response helped song lyrics stay alive and reach across local and state boundaries. A particular song leader was often so prominent and gifted that a song would initially be called "Brother or Sister So-and-So's song." After he or she was gone, the piece was no longer sung. By incorporating the words from the spiritual into this medley, Donnie McClurkin has ensured that this piece is not lost to the church today.

The second part of the medley, beginning with "Living He loved me," is from a hymn called "One Day," which was copyrighted in 1910. J. Wilbur Chapman (1859–1918) wrote the words to this hymn and Charles H. Marsh (1859–1956) wrote the music.

Finally, the verses beginning with "Send Him on down" are typical of choruses from the early 1900s when the Pentecostal influence became a strong factor in sacred music. In fact, these very verses are still sung regularly in Pentecostal services today.

"Church Medley" is a great illustration of the contemporary trend in gospel music of gathering together many of the old psalms, hymns, and spiritual songs and then arranging them in a contemporary style. I have personally led the performance of this song many times. One time was especially meaningful to me. It was in December 1994, while I was minister of music with Times Square Church, and I was leading the choir in an appearance at the famous tree-lighting ceremony at Rockefeller Center in New York City. Thousands of people around that skating rink heard this great message of the gospel, some for the first time. As a result, we received phone calls from churches and individuals all around the country asking for the music. We even had a call from the principal of a Catholic school who wanted his school choir to learn and perform this piece. For me, it was a sweet reminder of the universal appeal of this medley, and of the different types of songs it contains.

Give Me a Clean Heart

Words and Music by Margaret J. Douroux

Chorus

Give me a clean heart so I may serve Thee. Lord, fix my heart___ so that I___ may be used___ by Thee. For I'm not wor - thy of all these

bless - ings. Give me a clean heart____

____ and I'll fol - low Thee._____ 1. I'm not

ask - ing for the rich - es of the land.____

clean heart, a clean heart and I will fol - low

Thee. _____ 2. Some - times _____

1.

2.

rit.

pp

2. *Sometimes I am up and sometimes I*
   am down.
   Sometimes I am almost level to the
   ground.
   Please give me, Lord, a clean heart,

That I may follow Thee.
Give me a clean heart, a clean
   heart
And I will follow Thee.

*M*argaret Pleasant Douroux was born in 1941, and today is known as a distinguished composer, arranger, and publisher of gospel music, hymns, anthems, and spirituals, having penned over a hundred compositions. She founded and serves as president of the Reverend Edward A. Pleasant Publishing Company, and has published such books as *About My Father's Business* (1977), *Christian Principles That Motivate and Enhance Education Among Black Children* (1979), and *Find the Kingdom* (1985). Among her notable music recordings are *Revival from the Mount* (1970), *The Way of the Word* (1982), and *Signs of Advent* (1987). Douroux is also founder and CEO of Heritage Music Foundation and serves as minister of music at New Bethel Baptist Church in Los Angeles. Her songs have been recorded by singers such as the Mighty Clouds of Joy, the Gospel Music Workshop of America, and writer/poet Nikki Giovanni.

The title of this song, "Give Me a Clean Heart," is the request made repeatedly throughout these verses and the chorus. That very request is Margaret's focus here, the message of the song. And yet it is interesting to note that, in the midst of her humility ("I'm not worthy of all these blessings"), she comments indirectly on the social and cultural status of the times: "I'm not asking for the riches of the land. I'm not asking for the proud to know my name." Although these lines are in keeping with the author's expression of humility, they also seem to indicate the ongoing struggle of the African-American for success and recognition, both materially and socially. "Sometimes I am up and sometimes I am down. Sometimes I am almost level to the ground" is a "wandering verse" from the slave spiritual era. It was used in "Nobody Knows de Trouble I've Seen" and many others. These statements, of course, can be said of anyone at different times of life. And yet, looking back over the history of the African-American, the struggle seems to echo down through the centuries with so much more feeling and authenticity than with any other race of people.

"Give me a clean heart" is the refreshing, selfless request of one who is able to look beyond the pain of the past and the continuing struggle of the present to a future full of promise, a life of much deeper meaning than anything that can be achieved on earth. It calls to mind a similar request by King David in Psalm 51:10: "Create in me a clean heart, O God, And renew a steadfast spirit within me."

God Is

Words and Music by Robert J. Fryson

God___ is___
He, He is my___ all___ and all. 2. God

Chorus

God is the joy and the strength of my life.___ He

moves all pain, mis - er - y and strife. He

pro - mised to keep___ me, nev - er to leave___ me. He

nev - er ev - er comes short of his word. I have to

fast and pray,— stay in the nar - row way,— com -

mit my life— clean ev - 'ry day.— I

want to go with— Him when He comes back.— I've

come too far— and I'll nev - er turn back.

God is, God is, God is, God is,

2. *God is my joy in the time of*
   sorrow.
 Oh, God is my all and all.

God is my today and my tomorrow.
Oh, God is—He is my all and all.

uthor Robert J. Fryson has titled his song as simply and yet profoundly as possible—"God Is"—a two-word sentence that sums up not only the songs of the African-American church but of all of Christendom as well. "God is." It is reminiscent of God's response to Moses when the patriarch asked God's name. God said simply, "I am." "God is" is a statement of faith that carried the slaves through the most torturous and shameful time in America's history. It is a statement of faith out of which the spirituals were born. It is a statement of faith that was the mainstay of the hush harbor meetings, where believers continued to gather together despite the very real dangers of doing so.

"God is" carried the emancipated African-Americans through the difficulties and disappointments of the Reconstruction and post-Reconstruction periods, the migration to the North, the deprivation and losses of the depression. And it became the heart of gospel music, both historic and modern. As African-Americans progressed through the civil rights struggles of the 1950s and '60s, "God is" was the cry of their freedom songs. For inherent in that statement was the declaration that, because God is, we have hope, we have purpose, we have dignity—and someday we will be free.

It is no wonder, then, that in spite of what Wyatt T. Walker, in his book *Somebody's Calling My Name,* refers to as "repeated broken faith, undisguised oppression, and rampant injustice," the African-American community continues to return, as it always has, to the religion of its forebears. The God who is today is the same God who sustained a race of people in the most difficult of times. History, therefore, is our witness that He will still be God in the ages to come.

The power of this simple song of praise was brought home to me one day recently. It was a Saturday in the spring of 1994, when I was pastor to the music ministry of Times Square Church. The choir and band had gone out on an evangelistic outreach to Washington Square Park by the New York University campus. We wanted to reach the students before the semester was over, as well as community residents and the indigents who often slept in the park. It was a very successful outreach. Members of the band and choir gave testimonies of being delivered from drug and alcohol addiction and prostitution, and the listeners responded well. When we asked people to come forward and turn their lives over to Jesus, several came. Then, as we were about to close the service, Brother Fred, the bass player, suggested we close out with "God Is." Brother Arthur, composer of "To You, Jesus," began to sing. Suddenly people streamed forward in droves, seeking prayer and counsel, receiving salvation and deliverance. Brother Arthur's favorite line from this song is "God is my all and all." Many people discovered that great truth that Saturday in the park.

My Tribute

Words and Music by Andrae Crouch (born 1950)

How_____ can I say thanks for the things You have done for me? Things_____ so un-de-served, yet You gave_____ to prove Your

love for me. The voic-es of a mil-lion an-gels could not ex-

press my grat-i - tude; All that I am and ev-er hope to

be, I owe it all to Thee. To

pleas - ing — Lord, to Thee; — And should I gain   an-y

praise,   Let it go to Cal - va - ry.   With His

blood   He has saved   me,   With His pow'r   He has

*M*y Tribute" is one more of the many well-known songs written and sung by Andrae Crouch. It is appropriate that someone as highly visible and successful in the music and entertainment industry as Crouch would be best known for this song in which he gives all credit for everything he has ever accomplished to God. Of course, he is not the first one to write a song in which all glory is given to God. It is highly possible that he was inspired by Fanny Crosby's hymn "To God Be the Glory":

> *To God be the glory, great things He hath done!*
> *So loved He the world that He gave us His Son,*
> *Who yielded His life an atonement for sin,*
> *And opened the Life-gate that all may go in.*

> *Praise the Lord, Praise the Lord,*
> *Let the earth hear His voice!*
> *Praise the Lord, Praise the Lord,*
> *Let the people rejoice!*
> *O come to the Father through Jesus the Son,*
> *And give Him the glory, great things He hath done.*

Andrae Crouch's musical style combines elements of ballad, rock, country, and soul with traditional gospel sounds. As early as the 1970s he was incorporating electronic instruments, including synthesizers, into his bands. The awards and accolades that have fallen on him are countless, but the humility in Andrae's music is evident, particularly as he sings, "If I gain any praise, Let it go to Calvary [the place where Jesus was crucified]." Although Andrae's popularity has spanned several decades and shows no signs of waning, he is obviously a man who has not let fame or success cloud his vision. Possibly the reason is that his focus is not on himself, and his style is timeless. As he says, "I don't listen to what's out there and try to make myself different. I'm just doing what I do and treating a song the way I feel it should be treated. I don't like trendy things. It makes you dated."

O Happy Day

Music by Edwin Hawkins (born 1943)
Words by Philip Doddridge (1702–1751)

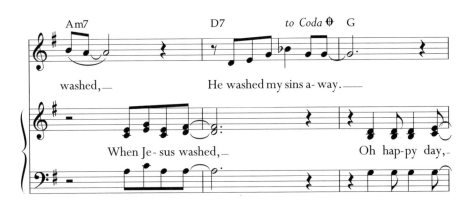

washed,—   He washed my sins a-way.—

When Je-sus washed,—   Oh hap-py day,-

Oh hap-py day!

Oh hap-py day!—

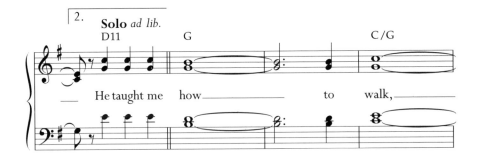

2. **Solo** *ad lib.*

He taught me how——   to   walk,——

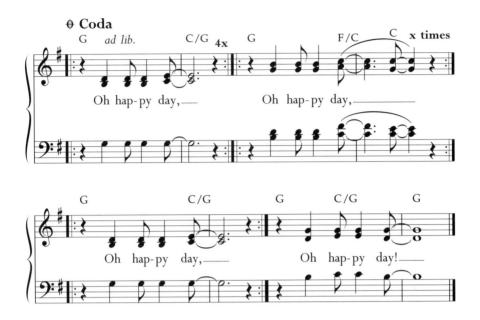

$\mathscr{I}$t is obvious that this beautiful hymn by Philip Doddridge deeply influenced the popular and powerful gospel song of one of the best-known and
most gifted songwriters of our day, Edwin Hawkins. Born into a family of
twenty children, Philip Doddridge lost both his parents before he completed grammar school. His firm biblical foundation had already been established at his mother's knee, however, and he grew up to be a renowned
minister, as well as the head of an academy where he trained over two
hundred young men for the ministry. Doddridge is highly respected as a
composer, ranked along with Isaac Watts and Charles Wesley as one of
England's finest eighteenth-century hymn writers.

Edwin Hawkins, born almost two centuries after Doddridge's death,
shared his predecessor's passion for singing this great testimony to the joy
of sins forgiven. Hawkins founded his first gospel group in 1967. It consisted primarily of members of his father's Holiness church, and their original purpose was to perform at the Annual Youth Congress of the Church
of God in Christ (COGIC) in Washington, D.C. The group was so suc-

cessful that they decided to become a permanent group, calling themselves the Northern California State Youth Choir. In 1968 they changed their name to the Edwin Hawkins Singers. Their recording of "O Happy Day" the following year brought them wide attention and greatly helped to establish them among the leading gospel groups of the time.

The Edwin Hawkins Singers toured throughout the United States and abroad, appearing not only in churches but also on television and radio, on college campuses, and in concert halls. Since that time, the group has produced several albums, including *Children Get Together* and *Love Alive II,* and has received many awards from the music and recording industries.

As is typical of the various types of sacred music included in this book, "O Happy Day" carries a timeless, universal message. This was powerfully brought home to me recently as a friend named Kathi was sharing with me the impact of this song on her life. In 1974, at the age of twenty-six and in the midst of a seemingly impossible situation, Kathi sat, despondent and alone, listening to a rock and roll station on the radio. Thinking of the things she had heard over the years about God, she decided to pray. Dropping to her knees, Kathi called out to God to forgive her for the mess she had made of her life and to give her a new start. As she felt the love of God wash over her, she suddenly heard the disk jockey's voice from the radio station she had been listening to. He said, "Here's a song I haven't played in a few years, but one that somebody needs to hear. You know who you are. This one's for you." And he played "O Happy Day," by the Edwin Hawkins Singers.

"I knew that song was for me," Kathi said. "It was God's reassurance to me that I was loved and forgiven. My life has never been the same."

This song was written years before the day it ministered to my friend, which shows its timelessness. And, although the group singing the song was black, Kathi is white, which shows its universal appeal and message.

Savior More Than Life

Words and Music by Kirk Franklin

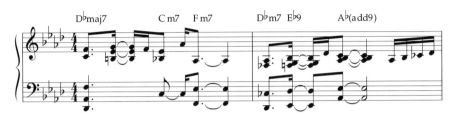

Chorus

Sav - ior, more— than life to me,— You

are the joy— and air I breathe.— No oth - er love— shall there be,— that

You are,— Lord, You're more than life.—

You— are more— than life to me. Yes, You are!—

That is why— I love You so.—

That is why— I love You so.—

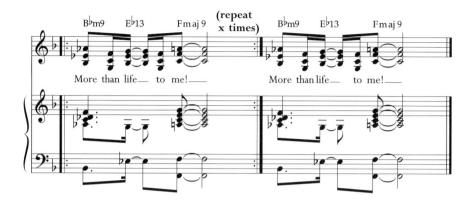

On his recent album, Kirk Franklin and the Family's *Whatcha Lookin' 4,* Franklin opens up with this composition based on a favorite hymn by Fanny Crosby titled "Savior, More Than Life to Me." The old hymn continues the opening line with, "I am clinging, clinging close to Thee." Franklin, too, like the former songwriter, expresses with loving gratitude his great need for the God who is his all in all, the very breath he breathes. Also included in this album are songs such as "When I Think About Jesus," the traditional gospel shouting song, and the well-known hymn "Jesus Paid It All," set to Franklin's musical arrangement. His gloriously lyrical song of thanksgiving, "Washed Away," is sung at times a cappella and with the typical African-American ad-lib style, while looking back to the style of the spirituals of old in harmony, vocal texture, and rhythm.

Franklin's music has universal age appeal, bridging the gap between young and old. Until 1993 he was best known in gospel circles as a pianist and choir director, having started both of these careers at the age of ten. But then in 1993 his debut album, *Why We Sing,* was released on Gospo Centric Records, earning him countless awards, television appearances, and platinum success. Although his popularity continues to escalate, he did have a brief brush with near-tragedy on November 11, 1996. While leaving the stage in Dallas to return to his dressing room, he was momentarily distracted and fell into a darkened orchestra pit. Thankfully, although he sustained head injuries and was unconscious for a time, he recovered quickly.

"At 5'2" and barely 130 pounds, I hardly have anything to sustain a big bang like that," Franklin said. "But God knew by sparing my life that I could be a better witness of what I'm singing about."

The recently married gospel singer and ordained minister has experienced great success with his music, particularly his album *Whatcha Lookin' 4*. In regard to the album title, Franklin says he believes that people "are looking for the type of satisfaction and love from relationships that can only come from a Christian experience." Franklin sings about that experience—and lives it as well.

Soon and Very Soon

Words and Music by Andrae Crouch (born 1950)

2. *No more cryin' there, we are going
   to see the King;*
   *No more cryin' there, we are going
   to see the King;*
   *No more cryin' there, we are going
   to see the King;*
   *Hallelujah! Hallelujah! We're
   going to see the King!*

3. *No more dyin' there, we are going
   to see the King;*
   *No more dyin' there, we are going
   to see the King;*
   *No more dyin' there, we are going
   to see the King;*
   *Hallelujah! Hallelujah! We're
   going to see the King!*

*T*he message of "Soon and Very Soon," by Andrae Crouch, has much in common with two of the historic gospels included in this book, "I'll Be Caught Up to Meet Him in the Air," by Clarence E. Hatcher, and "I'll Fly Away," by Albert E. Brumley. All three of these songs speak of looking forward to leaving this life behind and moving on to the next where King Jesus awaits.

In addition to the hope of a better life to come, there is a great universal appeal to Christians from all walks of life in this song, which declares, "We have come from every nation" and "God knows each of us by name." Not only do these lines symbolize the unity of those who believe in the same God and the same good news of the gospel message, but they stress the individuality and importance of each believer to God, in that He knows us by name. The King who is sung about in this song is not an impersonal God; He is one who cares enough to know each of His children by name.

There is great comfort in that to those who look forward to seeing Him one day. It is especially meaningful to those who may, for whatever reason, have been treated as unimportant in this lifetime. Whether struggling under the bondage of slavery or the deprivation of the depression, or marching in freedom marches in an attempt to gain the rights and privileges that are supposed to be possessed by all citizens of this country, African-Americans have had to fight to maintain their dignity. To be treated as second-class citizens—or, indeed, as less than citizens at all— only reinforces the need to be recognized as one with worth. In declaring that the King knows each of us by name, that worth is affirmed in a way no amount of human acceptance can bestow.

And that affirmation from God is much more important to Andrae Crouch than success and acceptance from the masses. With his long-standing success on the contemporary gospel scene, Andrae has a word of caution to other gospel singers when it comes to crossing over to the secular charts. "If you get too popular with too many people, you're not in touch with God. The devil will never shake hands with God. You can get out there, but they can't like you too much if you represent Jesus." For those gospel singers who have skyrocketed to secular stardom, he says, "I think they need to take a second look at some of their stuff. I like how people have accepted them but I think their focus is off. They'll be back as soon as they get focused."

Through It All

Words and Music by Andrae Crouch (born 1950)

Slowly and tenderly

1. I've had man-y tears and sor-rows,
I've had ques-tions for to-mor-row,

There've been times I did-n't know right from wrong;_____

But in ev - 'ry sit - u - a - tion God gave

bless - ed con - so - la - tion that my tri - als come to

on - ly make me strong.

Chorus

Through it all,

Through it all, Oh, I've

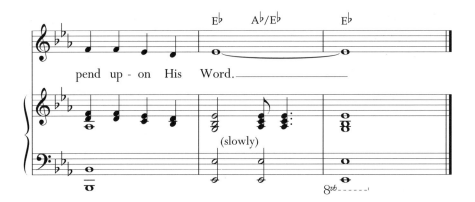

2. *I've been to lots of places,*
   And I've seen a lot of faces,
   There've been times I felt so all
      alone;
   But in my lonely hours,
   Yes, those precious lonely hours,
   Jesus let me know that I was His
      own.

3. *I thank God for the mountains,*
   And I thank Him for the valleys,
   I thank Him for the storms He
      brought me through;
   For if I'd never had a problem
   I wouldn't know that He could
      solve them,
   I'd never know what faith in God
      could do.

*T*hrough It All" is one of Andrae Crouch's best-known songs, and symbol-izes so well what he—and so many others—have found to be true through the years. Regardless of the inevitable hard times, God is always there to sustain us and carry us through. In Andrae's own words, "I am so grateful to the Lord for what He has done for me. . . . He has never forsaken me; He's always been there."

Andrae is truly a humble superstar on the contemporary gospel scene. When he wrote "My Tribute," he gave all the credit and glory to God for his accomplishments. But others in the business wanted to show Andrae just how much they loved and respected him and his work. And so, recently they got together and produced a recording titled *Tribute: The Songs of Andrae Crouch.* More than two years went into the making of this recording, and it features such well known contemporary artists as Michael W. Smith, Twila Paris, Bryan Duncan, Wayne Watson, Clay Crosse,

Take 6, the Brooklyn Tabernacle Choir, First Call, and the Winans. (The Winans—brother and sister, BeBe and CeCe—are currently one of the most popular music duos in both the gospel and secular markets. They have achieved gold and platinum albums, as well as Grammy, Stellar, and Dove awards.) Crouch was also honored at the twenty-seventh annual Dove Awards, where an all-star collection of artists came together and performed a medley of Andrae's original compositions.

Crouch's music has now been translated into twenty-one languages. His concerts are sellouts. He has won nine Grammy Awards and an Academy Award nomination. And his first album in a decade, *Mercy,* is another top-notch success. From the young boy who began singing in his father's church, Andrae Crouch has come a long way to the place where he is now considered a world-class artist whose music knows no boundaries.

To You, Jesus

Words and Music by Arthur Lee Freeman

Je - sus, I lift my hands— up to You,—

Je - sus I lift my life— up to You,—   Je - sus, I lift my

won - der - ful Je - sus, praise You.   Praise You,___   praise

You,___   won - der - ful Je - sus, praise You.

*A*rthur Freeman, the author of this song, was born in Langley, a suburb of Columbia, South Carolina, in the early 1940s. At the age of three he began to sing, mostly to the homeless, wayward, and poor families who showed up on his mother's front porch for a meal and a prayer. When he was five years old his family moved to Jersey City, New Jersey, where he grew up, eventually moving to New York City. Although his young years were marred by the hardship and heartache of his parents' divorce, the love of God and the affections of his older sisters healed him. Raised as a Baptist, Arthur later accepted an invitation to attend Refuge Temple Church of God in Christ. The excitement and exuberance of the praise and worship he witnessed there appealed to Arthur. Soon he was writing and singing for God. According to Freeman, this particular song "was written for my pastor, Gwendolin Sims Warren." I am deeply honored. Arthur's songwriting background is typical of one growing up in the era of the evolution of gospel—both historic and contemporary. He sang with the Teen Gospelaires, the Isaac Douglas Singers, the New York Community Choir, and a gospel/pop group called Revelation.

The words to "To You, Jesus" are simple and repetitive, but that very simplicity that gives the song its depth. Freeman has successfully stripped away all excess baggage—concern with self, personal needs or desires, distractions, preoccupations, outside relationships—and has focused on the one lasting thing that truly matters to him. He recognizes his own inability to offer anything of any worth to Jesus except himself, and so he does just that. Through the song's lyrics, Freeman offers up his hands, his life, his spirit, his praise, and his worship. In that complete offering lies the meaning of the term "a sacrifice of praise."

When the slaves stole away, under threat of dire consequences, to their hush harbor meetings to sing to and about God, they were indeed offering up a sacrifice of praise. For depression-era African-Americans, many of whom had no idea where their next meal was coming from, to sing of a faithful God who supplied all their needs was not only an act of faith but a sacrifice of praise as well. For anyone who is willing to declare—in song or otherwise—the willingness to offer up all earthly possessions, including life itself, to the only One who really matters, is truly offering up a sacrifice of praise. It is a sacrifice that has nothing to do with current situations or circumstances. It is a sacrifice that is offered up regardless of feelings. And it is a sacrifice that will ultimately be rewarded when God, to whom we sing, welcomes us home.

If there is one common thread we have seen running throughout all the hymns, spirituals, historic and modern gospels, it is this: each at its heart is sung to Jesus. There is a dedication to Christ that comes through in the words of every songwriter, a love for Him that is intensified for each singer and listener. "To You, Jesus" is such a beautiful expression of that love and dedication, as is another of Freeman's songs, "That's Reason Enough to Praise Him." Here is an excerpt from that song:

> *Are you looking for a reason to praise the Lord?*
> *Can you lift your hands without a doubt?*
> *Can you tell someone "He's been my Savior"?*
> *When trials come, He'll bring you out!*
>
> *He provides for me,*
> *when I'm in need,*
> *and that's reason enough to praise Him . . .*
>
> *God gave His only Son,*
> *to die on the cross,*
> *and that's reason enough to praise Him . . .*

Total Praise

Words and Music by Richard Smallwood

*T*otal Praise" is one of the songs recorded by Richard Smallwood with his new choir, Vision, on his 1996 album *Adoration: Live in Atlanta.* This album contains songs Smallwood has composed, such as "Bless the Lord," "Everything That Hath Breath," "Thank You," and "I Will Sing Praises." He has also included his arrangement of the old favorite traditional song "Great Day," which is included in the spirituals section of this book. All of the recordings on this album are typical of present-day gospel songs, which feature songs of praise and adoration.

Smallwood was breaking into—and helping to establish—contemporary gospel music at the time of some of the greatest civil rights struggles in the country, what we often think of as the Martin Luther King Jr. era, which was roughly from 1955 to 1968. King was born near the onset of the depression, on January 15, 1929. In the classic words of Lerone Bennett, author of *Before the Mayflower: A History of the Negro in America, 1619–1964,* King's commitment to his people as well as to nonviolent means of protest "moved the [civil rights] struggle from the courtroom to the streets, from law libraries to the pews of the churches, from the mind to the soul." King challenged America's conscience to a degree that few have done before or since.

How natural, then, that out of that struggle for freedom would come the freedom songs that would bridge the historic and contemporary gospel songs. Along with the freedom songs, Richard Smallwood has successfully made that transition. From one who made his mark during the beginning of the move from historic to contemporary gospel, he continues to enjoy ever-growing success in the music industry today.

Why We Sing

Words and Music by Kirk Franklin

Choir

1., 2. Some - one asked the ques - tion, Why do we sing? When we

lift our hands to Je - sus, What do we real - ly mean?

Glo - ry, Hal - le - lu - jah! You're the rea - son why— I sing.—

Coda

tell the whole— world. No!—   5. And when we cross— that ri - ver, To

stu - dy war— no more,— We will sing our songs— to Je - sus! The

rea- son why   I

*W*hy We Sing," a composition based on the hymn "His Eye Is on the Sparrow," is one of the songs on Kirk Franklin's 1993 album *Kirk Franklin and the Family*. This album was Franklin's first recording and is already an all-time best-seller. A brilliant, prolific young songwriter, Franklin was born and raised in Fort Worth, Texas. His teenage parents abandoned him when he was three, and he was adopted by a sixty-four-year old aunt named Gertrude Franklin. By the time Kirk was four he had started playing the piano, his aunt collecting aluminum cans to pay for his music lessons. This same aunt is the one who made sure he was in church every Sunday.

Franklin was offered his first recording contract when he was only seven years old, but his aunt thought he was too young. But by the time he was eleven he had been appointed minister of music at Mt. Rose Baptist Church. It was then that he began writing and arranging Christian music.

Though still in his early twenties, this successful young artist, who refers to his music not as gospel music but as "Christian Love music," has experienced more trials than many of us face in a lifetime. However, his unyielding faith has left him with a powerful testimony. A quote from his album insert reads: "God has blessed us with another gifted musical minister in Kirk Franklin. His lyrics are inspiring, his music uplifting, and his performance is anointed."

Another outstanding song on this album is "Silver and Gold," which looks back to George Beverly Shea's well-known hymn "I'd Rather Have Jesus." Franklin uses much the same phrases as Shea when he says, "I'd rather have Jesus, than silver or gold; I'd rather have Him, than riches untold." As with Franklin's other songs, "Silver and Gold" expresses clearly his priorities and his gratitude to God. As he explains it, his musical gift, combined with God's matchless gift of grace, is "Why We Sing."

And that, I believe, is why it is so appropriate to end this book with this particular song. We have discussed the social and cultural situations under which many of these songs were written. We have discussed authors' lives, the meaning of certain lyrics, the biblical roots of many of the songs, the development of the music, and even the controversies involved in that development. But all of that is secondary to why we really sing. We sing because we are happy and free in our faith. It is a happiness and freedom that transcends any persecution or problem that comes against us. It is a happiness and freedom that will carry us through any troubles or tribulations we might face in the future. It is a happiness and freedom that nothing—and no one—can take from us.

And so we shall sing—"ev'ry time we feel the Spirit."

Bibliography

Introduction

Songs of Zion: Supplemental Worship Resources 12. Nashville: Abingdon, 1981.

Walker, Wyatt T. *Somebody's Calling My Name.* Valley Forge, Pa.: Judson Press, 1979.

I. The Negro Spirituals

Holy Bible. New Living Translation. Wheaton, Ill.: Tyndale House Publishers, 1996.

Jubilee and Plantation Songs: Characteristic Favorites as sung by the Hampton Students, Jubilee Singers, Fisk University Students, and other concert companies. Boston: Oliver Ditson & Co., 1887.

Life Application Bible: The Living Bible. Wheaton, Ill.: Tyndale House Publishers, 1988.

Songs of Zion.

Blassingame, John W., ed. *Slave Testimony: Two Centuries of Letters, Speeches, Interviews, and Autobiographies.* Baton Rouge and London: Louisiana State University Press, 1977.

Boatner, Edward. *The Story of the Spirituals: 30 Spirituals and Their Origins.* Miami, Fla.: McAfee Music Publications, 1973 (by Belwin Mills, c/o CPP Belwin, Inc., Miami, Fla.).

Epstein, Dena J. *Sinful Tunes and Spirituals: Black Folk Music to the Civil War.* Champaign: University of Illinois Press, 1981.

Hausman, Gerald and Rodrigues, Kelvin. *African-American Alphabet.* New York: St. Martin's Press, 1996.

Higginsen, Vy. *This Is My Song! A Collection of Gospel Music for the Family.* New York: Crown Publishers, 1995.

Johnson, James Weldon and Johnson, J. Rosamund. *The Books of American Negro Spirituals.* New York: Da Capo Press, 1954.

Lovell, John Jr. *The Black Song: The Forge and the Flame.* New York: Macmillan, 1972.

Nelson, Angela M. S. "The Spiritual: In the Furnace of Slavery, a Lasting Musical Form Was Forged." *Christian History* 31, vol. X, no. 3 (1991)—*The Golden Age of Hymns.*

Raboteau, Albert J. *Slave Religion: The "Invisible Institution" in the Antebellum South.* New York: Oxford University Press, 1978.

Reagon, Bernice Johnson. *We'll Understand It Better By and By: Pioneering African American Gospel Composers.* Washington and London: Smithsonian Institution Press, 1992.

Sobel, Mechal. *Travelin' On: The Slave Journey to an Afro-Baptist Faith.* Princeton: Princeton University Press, 1979.

Southern, Eileen. *Greenwood Encyclopedia of Black Music, Biographical Dictionary of Afro-American and African Music.* Westport, Conn.: Greenwood Press, 1982.

Southern, Eileen. *The Music of Black Americans.* New York: W. W. Norton, 1971.

Still, William Grant and Goodwin, Ruby Berkley. *Twelve Negro Spirituals.* New York: Handy Brothers Music Co., 1937.

Walker, Wyatt T. *Somebody's Calling My Name.*

Whalum, Wendall Phillips. "From Folk to Philharmonic: The Spiritual as Mature Choral Composition." *Black World* (July 1974).

Work, John W. *American Negro Songs and Spirituals.* New York: Crown Publishers, 1988.

II. The Gospel Songs

Holy Bible. King James Version, *The Thompson Chain-Reference Bible,* 4th ed. Indianapolis: B. B. Kirkbride Bible Co., 1964.

Holy Bible. New King James Version. Nashville: Thomas Nelson, 1983.

Holy Bible. New Living Translation.

Yes, Lord! The Church of God in Christ Hymnal. Memphis: Church of God in Christ Publishing Board (in assoc. with Benson Co.), 1982.

Bailey, Albert Edward. *The Gospel in Hymns, Background and Interpretations.* New York: Charles Scribner's Sons, 1950.

Boyer, Horace C. "Thomas A. Dorsey, 'Father of Gospel Music,' An Analysis of His Contributions." *Black World* (July 1974): 20–28.

Duckett, Alfred. "An Interview with Thomas A. Dorsey." *Black World* (July 1974): 13–14.

Erbson, Wayne. *Mel Bay's Old Time Gospel Songbook.* Pacific, Mo.: Mel Bay Publications, 1993.

Higginsen, Vy. *This Is My Song!*

Keyes, Alan L. *Masters of the Dream: The Strength and Betrayal of Black America.* New York: William Morrow and Co., 1995.

Osbeck, Kenneth W. *Amazing Grace: 366 Inspiring Hymn Stories for Daily Devotions.* Grand Rapids: Kregel Publications, 1990.

Petrie, Phil. "The History of Gospel Music." *Gospel Industry Today* (February 1996).

Reagon, Bernice Johnson. *We'll Understand It Better By and By.*

Terry, Lindsay. *Stories Behind Popular Songs and Hymns.* Grand Rapids: Baker Book House, 1990.

Washington, James Melvin. *Conversations with God: Two Centuries of Prayers by African Americans.* New York: HarperCollins, 1994.

III. The Euro-American Hymns

Christian History.

Holy Bible. King James Version.

Holy Bible. New International Version. Grand Rapids: Zondervan Bible Publishers, 1988.

Holy Bible. New King James Version.

Holy Bible. New Living Translation.

Songs of Zion.

Bailey, Albert Edward. *The Gospel in Hymns: Background and Interpretations.*

Bradley, Ian. *The Book of Hymns.* Woodstock, N.Y.: Overlook Press, 1989.

Konkel, Wilbur. *Living Hymns Stories.* Salem, Oh.: Schmul Publishing Co., 1993.

Miller, Kevin A. "Silent String." *Christian History* 31, vol. X, no. 3, 1991.

Whalum, Wendell, from J. Wendell Mapson Jr. *The Ministry of Music in the Black Church.* Valley Forge, Pa.: Judson Press, 1984.

IV. Contemporary Gospel Songs

"From Religious Roots to the Pop Charts." *New York Times Television,* February 2, 1997.

Holy Bible. New King James Version.

Jones, Lisa C. "Are Whites Taking Gospel Music?" *Ebony,* July 1995.

Lincszy, Almeter D. "Kirk Franklin and the family 'Tour of Life' live on." *Amsterdam News* (New York).

Lovell, John Jr. *The Black Song.*

Petrie, Phil. "A Shakin' in the Gospel Music Industry House." *Gospel Industry Today,* January 1997.

Shepherd, Linda. "Andrae Crouch Is Back with *Mercy.*" *Charisma,* November 1994.

Walker, Wyatt T. *Somebody's Calling My Name.*

Washington, James Melvin. *Conversations with God.*

Index